BIRTH

A Guide for Prayer

by
Jacqueline Syrup Bergan
S. Marie Schwan

Take and Receive series

Saint Mary's Press
Christian Brothers Publications
Winona, Minnesota

Companion books are available in this Take and Receive series. Write to
Saint Mary's Press
702 Terrace Heights
Winona, MN 55987-1320

All scriptural excerpts are from *The Jerusalem Bible*. Copyright © 1966, by Darton, Longman & Todd, Limited, Doubleday & Company, Inc., used with permission of the publisher.

Selections from *The Spiritual Exercises of St. Ignatius*, translated by David L. Fleming, SJ (The Institute of Jesuit Sources, St. Louis, 1978), are reprinted with permission.

The prayer "Letting Go" on page 142 is from *Orientations, Vol. I: A Collection of Helps for Prayer*, by John Veltri (Loyola House, 1979). Reprinted with permission.

With special thanks to our typist, S. Christine Johnson.

Printed in the United States of America

Printing: 11 10 9 8

Year: 1996 95 94

ISBN 0-88489-170-4

To my children
John, Thomas, James
Barry, Bridget, Cynthia, Bart, Stacy
—Jackie

In grateful memory to Donald J. Green, CPPS
—Marie

Contents

Foreword

In his journey from conception through death, Jesus was just like us in everything except sin. Though fully divine as the Son of God, he is also fully human as son of Mary.

His human journey is the pattern for our own. And one of the most significant aspects of his journey was his openness to the Holy Spirit. So, the Scriptures speak of Jesus as "full of the Holy Spirit," as "conducted by the Spirit into the desert," as living "in the power of the Spirit," as one who "rejoiced in the Holy Spirit." He himself testified that the Spirit of the Lord was upon him and he assured us that God would give the Holy Spirit to those who ask.

As we contemplate the deep meaning of Jesus' birth, his call, and his outreach to those in need, we appreciate more and more the wonder of God entering so fully into our human condition. We appreciate, too, the power of the Holy Spirit in the life of Jesus and our own deep need to be open to the Spirit, for it is only through the Spirit's presence and power within us that we can pattern our lives after the life of Jesus.

This third volume in the Take and Receive series, called *Birth*, will help us to experience the power of the Holy Spirit leading us deeply into the mystery of Jesus and moving us to love Jesus and to follow him as his beloved disciples.

Victor H. Balke
Bishop of Crookston
Crookston, Minnesota

July 31, 1985
Feast of Saint Ignatius of Loyola

Cover Design

A "season of glad songs" has begun; throughout the Church is heard the murmur of prayer. Quietly, and in stillness, within the hearts of Christians everywhere, winter has given way to the vitality of spring—the coming of the Spirit.

Among the heralds of spring is the return and nesting of birds. From the days of ancient Israel even to our own times, birds have been symbolic, not only of our deep homing instincts, but also of our creative impulse and of our desire for transcendence.

Frequent allusions to doves are made throughout the Scriptures. In The Song of Songs, the dove announces spring; in Genesis, the olive-bearing dove indicates the end of the flood (Gen. 8:11). At the Baptism of Jesus, the presence of the dove initiates a new age of the Spirit (Mark 1:8).

The pair of doves on the cover of volume one, *Love*, represents God's call to love. The cover of volume two, *Forgiveness*, depicts the blessing and nurturing of God's unconditional and forgiving love. The design of the cover of this volume, *Birth*, symbolizes the creative Spirit of God hovering over our world, birthing new life.

The mourning dove calls: "Come then, my love . . . . For see, winter is past " (Song of Sol. 2:10–11).

The covers were designed by Donna Pierce Campbell, popular Minnesota artist, whose beauty and freshness of style mirrors the spirit of renewal that this guide for prayer hopes to serve.

Introduction

This guide for prayer was inspired by the spiritual hunger we witnessed during the past years as we conducted parish days of renewal throughout northwestern Minnesota.

People shared with us their need and eagerness for guidance and support in developing a personal relationship with God. Gradually we grew in the awareness that for too long the laity has been deprived of resources that are an integral part of the tradition of spirituality within the Church.

One treasure within this tradition is the Spiritual Exercises of Saint Ignatius. The Exercises were a response to the need of the laity in the sixteenth century and have only recently been discovered anew. In the light of Vatican II, with its emphasis on Scripture, interior renewal, and the emergence of the laity, the Exercises have received a new relevance.

As we endeavored to adapt the pattern of the Exercises to parish days of renewal, we discovered an approach for integrating personal prayer with life circumstances that is appropriate to the needs, language, and lifestyle of the laity.

Birth: A Guide for Prayer is the third of five projected volumes, each of which provides a series of Scripture passages with commentaries and suggested approaches to prayer. The theme of each volume directly correlates with a segment of the Exercises, though each book can be used independently of the others.

The first book in the Take and Receive series, *Love*, made use of the themes present in the Principle and Foundation of the Spiritual Exercises. Those themes were the affirmation of human creaturehood, indifference to all created things, and commitment. The guide centered on God's love, our total dependence on that love, and the call to respond in freedom to praise, reverence, and serve God.

The second volume, *Forgiveness*, correlated with the first week of the Spiritual Exercises of Saint Ignatius. The themes treated personal and collective sinfulness insofar as it is an obstacle to the receiving of God's love. Sin and sinner are considered in light of God's merciful and forgiving love.

Volume three, *Birth*, is oriented toward a personal discovery of the profound significance of the life of Christ as the paradigm of each one's passage into a way of living that incarnates the Spirit of Jesus in our world. We are invited to contemplate the earthly life of Jesus from his Incarnation throughout his public ministry.

As we contemplate the deep meaning of his birth, his call, and his outreach to those in need, we grow in appreciation for the wonder of God entering so fully into our human condition. We experience, stirring within ourselves, the call of grace to respond decisively to the longing deep within our hearts to know Jesus, to love him, and to follow him.

Written specifically as a support for solitary prayer, the guide can also serve as a resource for faith-sharing in small groups.

The series of guides makes no claim to be the Spiritual Exercises, nor to be a commentary on them. It is an attempt to make available a means of entering into the Christocentric dynamic of conversion found in the Exercises.

In committing this approach to prayer in writing, we hope that more people will be able to draw nourishment from the Word of God, experience God's unique love for them, and become aware of the particular intention God holds for each of them.

While we have attempted to be sensitive to the use of inclusive language in the commentaries and approaches to prayer, we have not been entirely consistent. We have been reluctant to make changes in the biblical text out of respect for the Word of God and for those people who may find such changes offensive.

Our prayer for those who use this guide is that they will be led by the spirit of Jesus into true spiritual freedom.

May the God of our Lord Jesus Christ, the Father of glory, give you a spirit of wisdom and perception of what is revealed, to bring you to full knowledge of him. • May he enlighten the eyes of your mind so that you can see what hope his call holds for you, what rich glories he has promised the saints will inherit • and how infinitely great is the power that he has exercised for us believers. (Eph. 1:17–19)

Jacqueline Syrup Bergan
S. Marie Schwan

August 15, 1985
Feast of the Assumption of Mary

Orientations

Lord, teach us to pray.   Luke 11:1

Prayer is our personal response to God's presence. We approach the Lord reverently with a listening heart. God speaks first. In prayer, we acknowledge the Divine presence and in gratitude respond to God in love. The focus is always on God and on what God does.

The following suggestions are offered as ways of supporting and enabling attentiveness to God's Word and our unique response.

A. DAILY PATTERN OF PRAYER

For each period of prayer, use the following pattern:

1. Preparation
+ Plan to spend at least twenty minutes to one hour in prayer daily. Though there is nothing "sacred" about sixty minutes, most people find that an hour better provides for the quieting of self, the entrance into the passage, and so on.
+ The evening before, take time to read the commentary as well as the Scripture passage for the following day. Just before falling asleep, recall the Scripture passage.

2. Structure of the Prayer Period
+ Quiet yourself; be still inside and out. Relax. Breathe in deeply, hold your breath to the count of four, then exhale slowly through your mouth. Repeat several times.
+ Realize you are nothing without God; declare your dependency.
+ Ask God for the grace you want and need.
+ Read and reflect on your chosen scriptural passage, using the appropriate form, for example, meditation for poetic and nonstory passages, contemplation for story-event passages, and so on. See "Forms of Solitary Prayer," page 2.

+ Close the prayer period with a time of conversation with Jesus and his Father. Speak and listen. Conclude with an Our Father.

3. Review of Prayer

The review of prayer is a reflection at the conclusion of the prayer period. The purpose of the review is to heighten our awareness of how God has been present to us during the prayer period.

The review focuses primarily on the interior movements of consolation and desolation as they are revealed in our feelings of joy, peace, sadness, fear, ambivalence, anger. Often it is in the review that we become aware of how God has responded to our request for a particular grace.

Writing the review provides for personal accountability and is a precious record of our spiritual journey. To write the review is a step toward self integration.

In the absence of a spiritual director or a spiritual companion, the writing helps fill the need for evaluation and clarification. If one has a spiritual director, the written review offers an excellent means of preparing to share one's prayer experience.

Method: In a notebook or journal, after each prayer period, indicate the date and the passage. Answer each of the following questions:
+ Was there any word or phrase that particularly struck you?
+ What were your feelings? Were you peaceful? loving? trusting? sad? discouraged? What do these feelings say to you?
+ How are you more aware of God's presence?
+ Is there some point to which it would be helpful to return in your next prayer period?

B. FORMS OF SOLITARY PRAYER

There are various forms of scriptural prayer. Different forms appeal to different people. Eventually, by trying various methods, we become adept at using approaches that are appropriate to particular passages and are in harmony with our personality and needs.

This guide will make use of the following forms:

1. Meditation

In meditation one approaches the Scripture passage like a love letter; this approach is especially helpful in praying poetic passages.

Method:
+ Read the passage slowly, aloud or in a whisper, letting the words wash over you and savoring them.
+ Stay with the words that especially catch your attention; absorb them the way the thirsty earth receives the rain.
+ Keep repeating a word or phrase, aware of the feelings that are awakened.
+ Read and reread the passage lovingly as you would a letter from a dear friend, or as you would softly sing the chorus of a song.

2. Contemplation

In contemplation, we enter into a life event or story passage of Scripture. We enter into the passage by way of imagination, making use of all our senses.

Theologians tell us that through contemplation we are able to "recall and be present at the mysteries of Christ's life" (26, p. 149).

The Spirit of Jesus, present within us through Baptism, teaches us, just as Jesus taught the apostles. The Spirit recalls and enlivens the particular mystery into which we enter through prayer. Just as in the Eucharist the Risen Jesus makes present the paschal mystery, in contemplation he brings forward the particular event we are contemplating and presents himself within that mystery.

Method: In contemplation, one enters the story as if one were there.
+ Watch what happens; listen to what is being said.
+ Become part of the mystery; assume the role of one of the persons.
+ Look at each of the individuals; what does he or she experience? To whom does each one speak?
+ What difference does it make for my life, my family, for society, if I hear the message?

3

In the gospel stories, enter into dialogue with Jesus.

+ *Be there* with him and for him.
+ *Want him;* hunger for him.
+ *Listen* to him.
+ *Let him* be for you what he wants to be.
+ *Respond to him* (72, pp. 5-6).

3. Centering Prayer

"In centering prayer we go beyond thought and image, beyond the senses and the rational mind to that center of our being where God is working a wonderful work" (59, p. 28).

Centering prayer is a very simple, pure form of prayer, frequently without words; it is an opening of our hearts to the Spirit dwelling within us.

In centering prayer, we spiral down into the deepest center of ourselves. It is the point of stillness within us where we most experience being created by a loving God who is breathing us into life. To enter into centering prayer requires a recognition of our dependency on God and a surrender to God's Spirit of love.

"The Spirit too comes to help us in our weakness . . . the Spirit . . . expresses our plea in a way that could never be put into words . . ." (Rom. 8:26).

The Spirit of Jesus within us cries out "Abba, Father!" (Rom. 8:15).

Method: "Pause a while and know that I am God . . ." (Ps. 46:10).

+ Sit quietly, comfortable and relaxed.
+ Rest within your longing and desire for God.
+ Move to the center within your deepest self. This movement can be facilitated by imaging yourself slowly descending in an elevator, or walking down flights of stairs, or descending a mountain, or going down into the water, as in a deep pool.
+ In the stillness, become aware of God's presence; peacefully absorb God's love.

4. Mantra

One means of centering prayer is the use of the "mantra" or "prayer word." The mantra can be a single word or a phrase. It may be a word from Scripture or one that arises spontaneously from within your heart. The word or phrase represents, for you, the fullness of God.

Variations of the mantra may include the name "Jesus" or what is known as the Jesus prayer, "Lord, Jesus Christ, Son of the living God, have mercy on me, a sinner."

Method: The word or phrase is repeated slowly within oneself in harmony with one's breathing. For example, the first part of the Jesus prayer is said while inhaling; the second half, while exhaling.

5. Meditative Reading
"I opened my mouth; he gave me the scroll to eat • and said, '. . . feed and be satisfied by the scroll I am giving you.' I ate it, and it tasted sweet as honey" (Ezek. 3:2–3).

One of the approaches to prayer is a reflective reading of Scripture or other spiritual writings.

Spiritual reading is always enriching to our life of prayer. The method described below is especially supportive in times when prayer is difficult or dry.

Method: The reading is done slowly, pausing periodically to allow the words and phrases to enter within you. When a thought resonates deeply, stay with it, allowing the fullness of it to penetrate your being. Relish the word received. Respond authentically and spontaneously as in a dialogue.

6. Journaling
"If you read my words, you will have some idea of the depths that I see in the mystery of Christ" (Eph. 3:4).

Journaling is meditative writing. When we place pen on paper, spirit and body cooperate to release our true selves.

There is a difference between journaling and keeping a journal.

To journal is to experience ourselves in a new light as expression is given to the fresh images which emerge from our subconscious. Journaling requires putting aside preconceived ideas and control.

Meditative writing is like writing a letter to one we love. Memories are recalled, convictions are clarified, and affections well up within us. In writing we may discover that emotions are intensified and prolonged.

Because of this, journaling can also serve in identifying and healing hidden, suppressed emotions such as anger, fear, and resentment.

Finally, journaling can give us a deeper appreciation for the written word as we encounter it in Scripture.

Method: There are many variations for the use of journaling in prayer. Among them are the following:

+ writing a letter addressed to God;
+ writing a conversation between oneself and another (The other may be Jesus, or another significant person. The dialogue can also be with an event, an experience, or a value. For example, death, separation, or wisdom receives personal attributes and is imaged as a person with whom one enters into conversation);
+ writing an answer to a question, for example, "What do you want me to do for you?" (Mark 10:51) or "Why are you weeping?" (John 20:15);
+ allowing Jesus or another scripture person to "speak" to us through the pen.

7. Repetition

"I will remain quietly meditating upon the point in which I have found what I desire without any eagerness to go on till I have been satisfied" (Saint Ignatius of Loyola; 72, p. 110).

Repetition is the return to a previous period of prayer for the purpose of allowing the movements of God to deepen within one's heart.

Through repetitions, we fine-tune our sensitivities to God and to how God speaks in our prayer and within our life circumstances. The prayer of repetition allows for the experience of integrating who we are with who God is revealing himself to be for us.

Repetition is a way of honoring God's word to us in the earlier prayer period. It is recalling and pondering an earlier conversation with one we love. It is as if we say to God, "Tell me that again; what did I hear you saying?"

In this follow-up conversation or repetition, we open ourselves to a healing presence that often transforms whatever sadness and confusion may have been experienced in the first prayer.

In repetitions, not only is the consolation (joy, warmth, peace) deepened, but the desolation (pain, sadness, confusion) is frequently brought to a new level of understanding and acceptance within God's plan for us.

Method: The period of prayer that we select to repeat is one in which we have experienced a significant movement of joy or sadness or confusion. It may also be a period in which nothing seemed to happen, due, perhaps, to our own lack of readiness at the time.

+ Recall the feelings of the first period of prayer.
+ As a point of entry, use the scene, word, or feeling that was previously most significant.
+ Allow the Spirit to direct the inner movements of your heart during this time of prayer.

C. SPIRITUAL PRACTICES AND HELPS

1. Examen of Consciousness
"Yahweh, you examine me and know me . . ." (Ps. 139:1).

The examen of consciousness is the instrument by which we discover how God has been present to us and how we have responded to that presence through the day.

Saint Ignatius believed this practice was so important that, in the event it was impossible to have a formal prayer period, he insisted that the examen would sustain one's vital link with God.

The examen of consciousness is not to be confused with an examination of conscience in which penitents are concerned with their failures. It is, rather, an exploration of how God is present within the events, circumstances, feelings of our daily lives.

What the review is to the prayer period, the examen is to our daily life. The daily discipline of an authentic practice of the examen effects the integrating balance which is essential for growth in relationship to God, to self, and to others.

7

The method reflects the "dynamic movement of personal love: what we always want to say to a person whom we truly love in the order in which we want to say it. . . . Thank you. . . . Help me. . . . I love you. . . . I'm sorry. . . . Be with me" (18, pp. 34-35).

Method: The following prayer is a suggested approach to examen. The written response can be incorporated into the prayer journal.

+ God, my creator, I am totally dependent on you. Everything is a gift from you. *All is gift.* I give you thanks and praise for the gifts of this day. . . .

+ Lord, I believe you work through and in time to reveal me to myself. Please give me an increased awareness of how you are guiding and shaping my life, as well as a more sensitive awareness of the obstacles I put in your way.

+ You have been present in my life today. Be near, now, as I reflect on these things:
  your presence in the *events* of today . . .
  your presence in the *feelings* I experienced today . . .
  your *call* to me . . .
  my *response* to you. . . .

+ God I ask your loving forgiveness and healing. The particular event of this day that I most want healed is. . . .

+ Filled with hope and a firm belief in your love and power, I entrust myself to your care, and strongly affirm. . . . (Claim the gift you most desire, most need; believe that God desires to give you that gift.)

2. Faith-Sharing

"For where two or three meet in my name, I shall be there with them" (Matt. 18:20).

In the creation of community, members must communicate intimately with each other about the core issues of their lives. For the Christian, this is faith-sharing and is an extension of daily solitary prayer.

A faith-sharing group is not a discussion group, not a sensitivity session nor a social gathering. Members do not come together to share and receive intellectual or theological insights. Nor is the purpose of faith-sharing the accomplishment of some predetermined task.

The purpose of faith-sharing is to listen and to be open to God, who continues to reveal himself in the Church community represented in the small group which comes together in God's name. The fruit of faith-sharing is the "building up" of the Church, the Body of Christ (Eph. 4:12).

The approach to faith-sharing is one of reading and reflecting together on the Word of God. Faith-sharing calls us to share with each other, out of our deepest center, what it means to be a follower of Christ in our world today. To authentically enter into faith-sharing is to come to know and love each other in Christ whose Spirit is the bonding force of community.

An image that faith-sharing groups may find helpful is that of a pool into which pebbles are dropped. The group gathers in a circle imaging themselves around a pool. Like a pebble being gently dropped into the water, each one offers a reflection—his or her "word" from God. In the shared silence, each offering is received. As the water ripples in concentric circles toward the outer reaches of the pool, so too this word enlarges and embraces, in love, each member of the circle.

Method: A group of seven to ten members gathers at a prearranged time and place.

+ The leader calls the group to prayer and invites them to some moments of silent centering, during which they pray for the presence of the Holy Spirit.
+ The leader gathers their silent prayer in an opening prayer, spontaneous or prepared.
+ One of the members reads a previously chosen scriptural passage on which participants have spent some time in solitary prayer.
+ A period of silence follows each reading of the Scripture.
+ The leader invites each one to share a word or phrase from the reading.
+ Another member rereads the passage; this is followed by a time of silence.
+ The leader invites those who wish, to share simply how this passage personally addresses them, for example, by challenging, comforting, inviting.
+ Again the passage is read.
+ Members are invited to offer their spontaneous prayer to the Lord.
+ The leader draws the time of faith-sharing to closure with a prayer, a blessing, an Our Father, or a hymn.

+ Before the group disbands, the passage for the following session is announced.

3. The Role of Imagination in Prayer

Imagination is our power of memory and recall which makes it possible for us to enter into the experience of the past and to create the future. Through images we are able to touch the center of who we are and to surface and give life and expression to the innermost levels of our being.

The use of images is important to our psycho-spiritual development. Images simultaneously reveal multiple levels of meaning and are therefore symbolic of our deeper reality.

Through the structured use of active imagination, we release the hidden energy and potential for wholeness which is already present within us.

When we use active imagination in the context of prayer, and with an attitude of faith, we open ourselves to the power and mystery of God's transforming presence within us.

Because Scripture is, for the most part, a collection of stories and rich in sensual imagery, the use of active imagination in praying Scripture is particularly enriching.

Through imaging Scripture we go beyond the truth of history to discover the truth of the mystery of God's creative Word in our lives (22, p. 76).

4. Coping with Distractions

Do not become overly concerned or discouraged by distractions during prayer. Simply put them aside and return to your prayer material. If and when a distraction persists, it may be a call to attend prayerfully to the object of the distraction. For example, an unresolved conflict may well continue to surface until it has been dealt with.

Prayer of Love and Praise

Lord my God, when Your love spilled over
            into creation
                        You thought of me.
                        I am
from love   of love   for love.

Let my heart, O God, always
            recognize,
            cherish,
            and enjoy your goodness in all of creation.

Direct all that is me toward your praise.
Teach me reverence for every person, all things.
Energize me in your service.

                        Lord God
may nothing ever distract me from your
            love . . .
                        neither health nor sickness
                        wealth nor poverty
                        honor nor dishonor
                        long life nor short life.

May I never seek nor choose to be other
            than You intend or wish.   Amen.

Week I, Day 1: In Silence and Surrender

LUKE 1:26–38

In the sixth month the angel Gabriel was sent by God to a town in Galilee called Nazareth, • to a virgin betrothed to a man named Joseph, of the House of David; and the virgin's name was Mary. • He went in and said to her, "Rejoice, so highly favoured! The Lord is with you." • She was deeply disturbed by these words and asked herself what this greeting could mean, • but the angel said to her, "Mary, do not be afraid; you have won God's favour. • Listen! You are to conceive and bear a son, and you must name him Jesus. • He will be great and will be called Son of the Most High. The Lord God will give him the throne of his ancestor David; • he will rule over the House of Jacob for ever and his reign will have no end." • Mary said to the angel, "But how can this come about, since I am a virgin?" • "The Holy Spirit will come upon you," the angel answered, "and the power of the Most High will cover you with its shadow. And so the child will be holy and will be called Son of God. • Know this too: your kinswoman Elizabeth has, in her old age, herself conceived a son, and she whom people called barren is now in her sixth month, • for nothing is impossible to God." • "I am the handmaid of the Lord," said Mary, "let what you have said be done to me." And the angel left her.

"What good is it if Mary gave birth to the son of God fourteen hundred years ago and I do not also give birth to the Son of God in my time and culture?" (33, p. 221).

This question was the challenge addressed to a thirteenth-century parish by Meister Eckhart. A Dominican preacher as well as a theologian and mystic, Meister Eckhart insisted that at every moment God is giving birth to Jesus in all of creation.

The question, then, is our own, "What good is it to us if God was born at Bethlehem on Christmas morning?" (32, p. 307).

Mary's annunciation becomes ours. We, too, are to give birth to Christ in our world today.

With Mary, we ask, "But how can this come about?" The unfolding drama of Mary's response in this passage gives us a model for how the birthing of Jesus takes place.

"Listen! You are to conceive and bear a son. . . ."

Mary's surrender in openness and freedom to the seed of God's Word within her is the archetype of our own birthing of Jesus. The depth of her inner silence provided the matrix for the tender nurturance of the new life conceived within her, the Word made flesh.

If we, as mature Christians, desire to birth Christ, the example of Mary can serve to guide us toward the essential interior attitudes of silence and surrender. Only in that silence and in that surrender can the unique expression and energy of Christ's life in our personal history and daily circumstance be released.

In spite of fear and unanswered questions, Mary moved into the unknown. Creation happens in surrender; in the letting go new life emerges.

Suggested Approach to Prayer: The Hovering Spirit

+ *Daily prayer pattern:* (See pages 1 and 2.)
I quiet myself and relax in the presence of God.
I declare my dependency on God.

+ *Grace:* I ask for the gift of awe and amazement before the mystery of God becoming human.

+ *Method:* Contemplation, as on page 3.
I see and consider the three persons of the Trinity, God our Creator, God the Son, and God the Holy Spirit, as they lovingly look upon our world.

I try to enter into the vision of our world as God sees it.

I see the struggle that exists, the compulsive aimlessness of killing, the addiction, the poverty and the despair of so many men and women. I see the injustice of some world leaders as they manipulate wealth and resources for power.

Within my vision are all the people of the earth: men, women, children, and all the colors and shades of humanity. Some are disabled, crippled. Some are strong and whole. Some are newborn, while others are old and diminishing. I see them all . . . those filled with tears, those overjoyed with happiness, those experiencing total alienation.

I envision within my heart God's great love and compassion for all. I image this love as it moves slowly, tenderly over the darkness of our world and its people. Through this love the force of God's powerful Spirit is ignited.

It is time, time for God to act, to rescue us from our blindness and self destruction, to bring us to fulfillment. God's plan, secret and mysterious, is about to be brought forth.

I stay with God's vision; I observe the angel Gabriel as he approaches Mary. With God, I wait for her response.

+ *Closing:* I let my heart speak to God of my deep gratitude for his compassionate love for all of humankind . . . for me.

I close with the Our Father.

+ *Review of Prayer:* I write in my journal the feelings, experiences, and insights that surfaced within me during this period of prayer.

Week I, Day 2: God's Total Gift

LUKE 1:26–38

In the sixth month the angel Gabriel was sent by God to a town in Galilee called Nazareth, • to a virgin betrothed to a man named Joseph, of the House of David; and the virgin's name was Mary. • He went in and said to her, "Rejoice, so highly favoured! The Lord is with you." • She was deeply disturbed by these words and asked herself what this greeting could mean, • but the angel said to her, "Mary, do not be afraid; you have won God's favour. • Listen! You are to conceive and bear a son, and you must name him Jesus. • He will be great and will be called Son of the Most High. The Lord God will give him the throne of his ancestor David; • he will rule over the House of Jacob for ever and his reign will have no end." • Mary said to the angel, "But how can this come about, since I am a virgin?" • "The Holy Spirit will come upon you," the angel answered, "and the power of the Most High will cover you with its shadow. And so the child will be holy and will be called Son of God. • Know this too: your kinswoman Elizabeth has, in her old age, herself conceived a son, and she whom people called barren is now in her sixth month, • for nothing is impossible to God." • "I am the handmaid of the Lord," said Mary, "let what you have said be done to me." And the angel left her.

Who is Jesus?

We are not the first to ask!

With regularity, in the Christian Scriptures, witnesses posed this question. Repeatedly we hear awestruck individuals ask, "Who is he?" (Luke 7:49; 9:9). We hear the crowds respond to the words and actions of Jesus with amazement, "Who is this man?" (Matt. 21:10).

Who is Jesus?

That is *the* question that undergirds all theological probings. Yet, for all the

15

merit of theological and intellectual insight, we are not content with doctrinal statements.

Who is Jesus?

The question is catalytic. It brings to the surface our deepest yearnings to "know" . . . to *experience* Jesus.

Given the world situation, its structural, moral breakdown and conflictual cultures, this is the question we most need to address, individually and collectively.

Who is Jesus?

The entire Gospel endeavors to bring us into the message and spirit of who Jesus is.

The "good news" is that "Jesus *is* Lord" (Rom. 10:9).

In Luke 1:26–38, the evangelist is particularly concerned with addressing the role and identity of Jesus.

The passage is extraordinarily rich. So much is happening: an angel comes, a virgin conceives. . . . It is like viewing a very detailed medieval tapestry. One can easily become enthralled with the intricate images and miss the intent and central focus of the passage.

What the reader needs to be mindful of is that Luke's intent is to make every facet of the passage clarify and support the central focus that Jesus is Lord from the first moment of his conception.

An angel appeared to Mary. It is the same angel Gabriel who announced to Zachariah the birth of John the Baptist, the forerunner of Jesus (Luke 1:11ff).

Luke has deftly drawn the parallels between John and Jesus. The similarities between the two annunciations are fivefold, and Luke holds them within the Old Testament tradition of annunciation experiences. Both contain the appearance of an angel, an experience of fear, a message from God, an objection, and a sign. The sign in these stories is a pregnancy and birth.

The events surrounding the conception of Jesus have been used by Luke to emphasize the extraordinariness of his birth in comparison to John's and thereby to definitively identify him as the Son of God.

While the similarities between the stories of John and Jesus give us information and insight, that which occurs outside the traditional pattern is the most significant. Raymond Brown identifies these distinctive aspects as the manner in which Jesus was conceived, the description of Jesus' future accomplishments, and the portrait of Mary, his mother (13, p. 292).

A reflection on these aspects leads us to the acknowledgment and amazement that—in Jesus—God has become present among us; Jesus' birth gives birth to our hope.

Suggested Approach to Prayer: The Message of an Angel

+ *Daily prayer pattern:* (See pages 1 and 2.)
I quiet myself and relax in the presence of God.
I declare my dependency on God.

+ *Grace:* I ask for the gift of awe and amazement before the mystery of God becoming human.

+ *Method:* Contemplation, as on page 3.
I image myself in Mary's home. I become aware of the time of day, the furnishings, the colors, the scents, all in great detail.

I assume the role of Mary or that of an observer—a neighbor, or a friend.

I see what Mary is doing. I visualize the expression on her face. I imagine what may be occupying Mary's thoughts and what her feelings are as her marriage to Joseph draws near.

I image the angel Gabriel and listen as he speaks to Mary. I enter into the dialogue between Mary and Gabriel, allowing myself to share in Mary's experience of fear . . . of questioning . . . of amazement.

I listen carefully to Gabriel's reassuring words as they are addressed to Mary.

I am with Mary at her moment of surrender.

+ *Closing:* I stay with Mary in joy, thanksgiving, wonder, and praise. I beg for the grace to know and to draw closer to Jesus.
I close with the Our Father.

+ *Review of Prayer:* I write in my journal the feelings, experiences, and insights that surfaced within me during this period of prayer.

17

Week I, Day 3: A New Creation

LUKE 1:26–38

In the sixth month the angel Gabriel was sent by God to a town in Galilee called Nazareth, • to a virgin betrothed to a man named Joseph, of the House of David; and the virgin's name was Mary. • He went in and said to her, "Rejoice, so highly favoured! The Lord is with you." • She was deeply disturbed by these words and asked herself what this greeting could mean, • but the angel said to her, "Mary, do not be afraid; you have won God's favour. • Listen! You are to conceive and bear a son, and you must name him Jesus. • He will be great and will be called Son of the Most High. The Lord God will give him the throne of his ancestor David; • he will rule over the House of Jacob for ever and his reign will have no end." • Mary said to the angel, "But how can this come about, since I am a virgin?" • "The Holy Spirit will come upon you," the angel answered, "and the power of the Most High will cover you with its shadow. And so the child will be holy and will be called Son of God. • Know this too: your kinswoman Elizabeth has, in her old age, herself conceived a son, and she whom people called barren is now in her sixth month, • for nothing is impossible to God." • "I am the handmaid of the Lord," said Mary, "let what you have said be done to me." And the angel left her.

While the miracle of John's birth to barren parents was a shock and surprise to the Hebron community, the virgin conception of Jesus is even more startling. In John's birth, God fulfilled the wish of Elizabeth and Zachariah for a child. The conception of Jesus, however, is described as the direct action and power of the Spirit, unexpected and unmediated by human generativity.

In Jesus something remarkably new happened!

18

God's Spirit, present at the moment of creation, became active again.

"Now the earth was a formless void, there was darkness over the deep, and God's Spirit hovered over the water" (Gen. 1:2).

Mary was overshadowed by God's creative spirit. She, however, was not barren; there was within her space to receive. She was free of distracting images and sterile idols. Within that purity of emptiness, receptivity was possible. Within the silent readiness, she welcomed the Word. She was transparent to God's creative action.

Be aware that any connotation of biological or sexual implications regarding the virginal conception of Jesus is totally inappropriate and without foundation. Teilhard de Chardin says:

> When the time had come when God resolved to realize His Incarnation before our eyes, He had first of all to raise up in the world a virtue capable of drawing Him as far as ourselves. He needed a mother who would engender Him in the human sphere. What did He do? He created the Virgin Mary, that is to say, He called forth on earth a purity so great that, within this transparency, He would concentrate Himself to the point of appearing as a child. (69, p. 114)

In this passage, Luke affirms the virginal conception of Jesus, "But it is set forth in order to explain something about Jesus" (29, p. 341).

". . . and will be called Son of God." These words and the image of the overshadowing Spirit remind us of the Baptism and transfiguration of Jesus. At Jesus' Baptism, the Spirit descended upon him, and we heard the words of the Creator, "This is my beloved Son" (Matt. 3:16–17; Mark 1:10–11; Luke 3:22). At his transfiguration, a cloud overshadowed Jesus and a voice declared "this is my beloved Son. . . . Listen to Him" (Matt. 17:5; Mark 9:7; Luke 9:34–35).

Luke has related to us the deep faith of the primitive church: Jesus' total life was under the influence of the Spirit and from the first moment of his human existence Jesus was truly God's Son.

Jesus is "the surprise of creation. No longer are we dealing with human request and God's generous fulfillment; this is God's initiative going beyond anything man or woman has dreamed of" (13, p. 314).

19

Suggested Approach to Prayer: Surrendering

+ *Daily prayer pattern:* (See pages 1 and 2.)
I quiet myself and relax in the presence of God.
I declare my dependency on God.

+ *Grace:* I ask for the gift of awe and amazement before the mystery of God becoming human.

+ *Method:* Centering and Mantra, as on page 4.
I become very quiet and still. I allow all previous images and distractions to fade away.

I listen to Gabriel as he tells me, "The Holy Spirit will come upon you, . . . and the power of the Most High will cover you with its shadow." I allow the words to enter deep within. I image myself being overshadowed by the presence of God's creative Spirit. I allow this presence to gently permeate my being.

I respond to this presence, making Mary's words of surrender my own: "I am the handmaid of the Lord, . . . let what you have said be done to me."

I stay with these words, using them as a mantra.

+ *Closing:* I stay with Mary in joy, thanksgiving, wonder, and praise. I beg for the grace to know and to draw closer to Jesus.
I close with the Our Father.

+ *Review of Prayer:* I write in my journal the feelings, experiences, and insights that surfaced within me during this period of prayer.

Week I, Day 4: Leap into Joy

LUKE 1:39–56

Mary set out at that time and went as quickly as she could to a town in the hill country of Judah. • She went into Zachariah's house and greeted Elizabeth. • Now as soon as Elizabeth heard Mary's greeting, the child leapt in her womb and Elizabeth was filled with the Holy Spirit. • She gave a loud cry and said, "Of all women you are the most blessed, and blessed is the fruit of your womb. • Why should I be honoured with a visit from the mother of my Lord? • For the moment your greeting reached my ears, the child in my womb leapt for joy. • Yes, blessed is she who believed that the promise made her by the Lord would be fulfilled."
And Mary said:

"My soul proclaims the greatness of the Lord and my spirit exults in God my savior;
because he has looked upon his lowly handmaid.
Yes, from this day forward all generations will call me blessed,
for the Almighty has done great things for me.
Holy is his name,
and his mercy reaches from age to age for those who fear him.
He has shown the power of his arm,
he has routed the proud of heart.
He has pulled down princes *from their thrones* and exalted the lowly.
The hungry he has filled with good things, *the rich sent empty away.*
He has come to the help of Israel his servant, mindful of his mercy

—according to the promise he made to our ancestors—
of his mercy to Abraham and to his descendants for ever."

• *Mary stayed with Elizabeth about three months and then went back home.*

Two mothers meet. They greet each other, and an energy of joy is awakened.

Jesus and John meet. Within the darkness and warmth of his mother's womb, John leaps for joy.

The meeting of Mary and Elizabeth serves as the vehicle for this first encounter of Jesus with John. The primary focus of the passage is the encounter and its significance.

The Hebrew Scriptures provide something of a precedent for the prenatal encounter of Jesus and John in the story of Esau and Jacob. As they "struggled with one another inside" their mother, Esau and Jacob set the tone of their life-long relationship (Gen. 25:22).

The prenatal meeting between John and Jesus was also prophetic. Not only did it presage the joy of their personal friendship, but it also served to unite them in a ministry which heralded a new age of reconciliation.

In the visit of Mary to Elizabeth there is a bridging, not of the Hebrew Scriptures to Christian Scriptures, but of the *extension* of the new to the old.

In the presence of Jesus, the hope of the Hebrew Scriptures is brought to completion in John's joy (John 3:29).

Jesus, himself, is the source of John's enthusiastic desire to awaken and prepare all humankind to receive the light, to receive Christ (John 1:7–8).

Mary carried this presence of Jesus to John.

Mary's relationship to Jesus speaks to us of what our own relationship with him can be. She carried and gave birth to his divine presence in our world. If we are also to carry and extend this presence, we can look to Mary.

"Yes, blessed is she who believed that the promise made to her by the Lord would be fulfilled."

Mary believed.

If there is one quality about Mary that most characterizes her, it is her

22

obedient trust in God. Within the ordinariness of her daily life, Mary was attentive and obedient to God's invitation to her as it was expressed in the needs of those around her. Her life was one of complete service and love. She heard the word of God within her and dared to act and trust in it. She lived in . . . "his trust in her trust in Him" (39, p. 17).

This trust was the essential element of the motherhood of Jesus. Jesus would say of her, "My mother and my brothers are those who hear the word of God and put it into practice" (Luke 8:21).

Amazingly, all of us are called to be mothers of God.

How will our "birthing" of Christ be experienced? The sign of its authenticity will be the joy effected in the lives of those we meet.

We must be swift to obey the winged impulses of His Love, carrying Him to wherever He longs to be; and those who recognize His presence will be stirred, like Elizabeth, with new life. They will know His presence, not by any special beauty or power shown by us, but in the way that the bud knows the presence of the light, by an unfolding in themselves, a putting forth of their own beauty. (39, p. 46)

New life is always an occasion for celebration. Luke places on Mary's lips a canticle of the early Church. In communion with Hannah (1 Sam. 2:1ff) Mary extols the holiness, power, and mercy of God. In this revolutionary hymn of praise, God is exalted as the one who favors those who put their trust totally in him, however materially or spiritually poor, oppressed, or politically weak they may be.

In cosmic unity, the entire universe—past, present, and future—sings and celebrates the blessings of our loving creator who in the birthing of Jesus fulfills the original promise of all ages.

In Jesus, the God of Abraham has met the Spirit of Mary, the Great Mother.

Suggested Approach to Prayer: In Silence and Joy

+ *Daily prayer pattern:* (See pages 1 and 2.)
  I quiet myself and relax in the presence of God.
  I declare my dependency on God.

+ *Grace:* I ask to know Jesus more intimately, to love him more intensely, to follow him more closely.

+ *Method:* Contemplation, as on page 3.

In the spirit of the visitation, I allow myself to return to my mother's womb. I relax in the experience of warmth and fluid security. I hear her voice as she speaks. I experience the rhythm of her walk. I am aware that my life is totally dependent on her very heartbeat. I allow myself to rest and to enjoy this sacred space of unity with creation.

I enter into the experience of John when Elizabeth was greeted by Mary. I image her words and the presence of Christ within her as a light, diffused and warmly glowing, enveloping my mother and myself.

I allow myself to respond, letting go of all former images, content with the space, the silence, and the joy of His presence.

+ *Closing:* I stay with Mary and offer joy, thanks, wonder, and praise. I beg for the grace to know and to draw close to Jesus.

I prayerfully read aloud the Magnificat.

+ *Review of Prayer:* I record my feeling response in my journal.

Week I, Day 5: A Timeless Birth

LUKE 2:1–14

Now at this time Caesar Augustus issued a decree for a census of the whole world to be taken. • This census—the first—took place while Quirinius was governor of Syria, • and everyone went to his own town to be registered. • So Joseph set out from the town of Nazareth in Galilee and travelled up to Judaea, to the town of David called Bethlehem, since he was of David's House and line, • in order to be registered together with Mary, his betrothed, who was with child. • While they were there the time came for her to have her child, • and she gave birth to a son, her first-born. She wrapped him in swaddling clothes, and laid him in a manger because there was no room for them at the inn. • In the countryside close by there were shepherds who lived in the fields and took it in turns to watch their flocks during the night. • The angel of the Lord appeared to them and the glory of the Lord shone around them. They were terrified, • but the angel said, "Do not be afraid. Listen, I bring you news of great joy, a joy to be shared by the whole people. • Today in the town of David a saviour has been born to you; he is Christ the Lord. • And here is a sign for you: you will find a baby wrapped in swaddling clothes and lying in a manger." • And suddenly with the angel there was a great throng of the heavenly host, praising God and singing:

> *"Glory to God in the highest heaven,*
> *and peace to [all] who enjoy his favour."*

joy . . . Joy . . . JOY!
"Listen, I bring you news of great joy, a joy to be shared by the whole people."

The news of great joy is the birthing of Christ—the birthing of God in our world and in ourselves. The good news is the universal cosmic gladness which is celebrated continually wherever new life and consciousness emerge.

This birthing is not limited by time or space. It reaches "from one end of the earth to the other . . ." (Wisd. 8:1) from the dawn of history to an eternal future.

Christ's coming in time celebrates the timelessness of this birthing. The coming of Christ in time points to and magnetically draws all of creation into a convergence of communion with Himself, who is, at once, the Alpha and the Omega (Rev. 22:13).

The longings and hopes of all generations and of all of life participate in and find fulfillment in his coming.

This cosmic significance of the birth of Christ is beautifully held and illuminated in Luke's rendering of the Christmas story. The story is a masterful integration of history, prophecy, and symbolism.

Luke begins his narration with the issuance of a "census of the whole world" by Augustus. The evangelist uses the occasion of a census to establish a setting for the birth of Jesus. Through the gathering together of all the people for registration, Luke conveys that the birth was to have significance for the "whole people." The census, which imposed oppressive taxation, further served to depict the political climate into which Christ was born.

Augustus, heralded as "father of peace," had, through military strategy, established a precarious détente throughout the Roman empire. Luke contrasts the false security offered by Augustus and the authentic saving power of Christ. The political maneuvering represented by Rome robbed the people of energy, of freedom, and of joy. The unexpected birth of Jesus upset the status quo so carefully engineered by Augustus.

The way and the power of Jesus dismantled and disrobed every instance of leadership which is based on false power, where those in authority "lord it over" others (Luke 22:25).

The birth of Jesus was a "decisive energizing toward a new social reality" (16, p. 97). The old categories, like old wineskins, were not adequate to hold this newness that Jesus brought.

How was the newness received?

"She wrapped him in swaddling clothes . . . ."

He was received with the warmth of a mother's love. Mary followed the prevailing custom which was to firmly wrap the newborn in swaddling bands. Although the primary purpose of such "swaddling" was to assure the straightness of the small limbs, it came to be associated with parental love and care. King Solomon said, "I was nurtured in swaddling clothes, with every care. No king has known any other beginning of existence" (Wisd. 7:4–5).

She "laid him in a manger because there was no room for them at the inn."

There was no room for them at the inn because the inn was not the appropriate place for the Son of God to be born. Luke recalled the words of Jeremiah addressed to God, "Yahweh, hope of Israel, / its saviour in time of distress, / why are you like a stranger in this land, / like a traveler who stays only for a night?" (Jer. 14:8).

The inn is the place where strangers and travelers rest for a brief time, perhaps overnight, as they pass through. Jesus had come to stay, to make his home among the people.

Tradition tells us that Jesus was born near Bethlehem in one of the caves which commonly served as dwelling and stable. The manger in which Luke says Jesus was laid draws its symbolic meaning from Isaiah 1:3: "The ox knows its owner / and the ass its master's crib, / Israel knows nothing. . . ."

Recognition of our Lord and master occurs only within the deepest recesses of one's self, there where one meets and is in touch with the roots of being.

The symbolism of cave and animals deeply draws us into the evolutionary experience of all birthing. It is within this primal place of the womb-like cave and among the animals that God's people come to recognize Jesus as their savior and their Lord.

The shepherds, whose life is centered in nature and the care of animals, were the first to receive the song of joy. Those nameless ones who lived on the fringes of society were the first to whom God birthed his son.

It is within those who have grieved loss, within those who know their own nothingness that Christ enters and transforms into his living presence.

They, like the shepherds, are the ones who are filled with the song of the angels singing, "Glory to God and peace to all who *enjoy* the gift of his birth."

Suggested Approach to Prayer: Within the Cave

+ *Daily prayer pattern:* (See pages 1 and 2.)
I quiet myself and relax in the presence of God.
I declare my dependency on God.

+ *Grace:* I ask to know Jesus more intimately, to love him more intensely and to follow him more closely.

+ *Method:* Contemplation, as on page 3.
I see Mary and Joseph as they travel from Nazareth to Bethlehem; I am aware of the discomfort of Mary, the concern of Joseph.

I enter the cave of Christ's birth. I allow myself to be immersed in the experience of his coming. I participate in his birthing in any manner in which I can serve.

I allow myself to be content within the amazement of this event. I open myself, in stillness, to absorb the joy of this happening.

+ *Closing:* I stay with Mary and Jesus, and offer joy, thanks, wonder, and praise, only begging for the grace to know and to draw yet closer to Jesus.

I pray the Our Father.

+ *Review of Prayer:* In my journal, I record my personal gratitude for the birthing of Christ.

Week I, Day 6: Repetition

Suggested Approach to Prayer

+ *Daily prayer pattern:* (See pages 1 and 2.)
I quiet myself and relax in the presence of God.
I declare my dependency on God.

+ *Grace:* I ask for the grace to know Jesus more intimately, to love him more intensely, and to follow him more closely.

+ *Method:* Reading "Repetition" on page 6 will be particularly helpful.
In preparation I review my prayer by reading my journal of the past week. I select for my repetition the period of prayer in which I was deeply moved. I proceed in the original manner, focusing on the scene, word, or feeling that was previously significant.

+ *Review of Prayer:* I write in my journal any feelings, experiences, or insights that have come to my awareness during this prayer period.

Week II, Day 1: The End of Waiting

LUKE 2:22–39

And when the day came for them to be purified as laid down by the Law of Moses, they took him up to Jerusalem to present him to the Lord—• observing what stands written in the Law of the Lord: Every first-born male must be consecrated to the Lord—• *and also to offer sacrifice, in accordance with what is said in the Law of the Lord,* a pair of turtledoves or two young pigeons. • *Now in Jerusalem there was a man named Simeon. He was an upright and devout man; he looked forward to Israel's comforting and the Holy Spirit rested on him. • It had been revealed to him by the Holy Spirit that he would not see death until he had set eyes on the Christ of the Lord. • Prompted by the Spirit he came to the Temple; and when the parents brought in the child Jesus to do for him what the Law required, • he took him into his arms and blessed God; and he said:*

> *• "Now, Master, you can let your servant go in peace, just as you promised;*
> *• because my eyes have seen the salvation*
> *which you have prepared for all the nations to see,*
> *• a light to enlighten the pagans*
> *and the glory of your people Israel."*

As the child's father and mother stood there wondering at the things that were being said about him, • Simeon blessed them and said to Mary his mother, "You see this child: he is destined for the fall and for the rising of many in Israel, destined to be a sign that is rejected—• and a sword will pierce your own soul too—so that the secret thoughts of many may be laid bare."

• There was a prophetess also, Anna the daughter of Phanuel, of the tribe of Asher. She was well on in years. Her

days of girlhood over, she had been married for seven years •
before becoming a widow. She was now eighty-four years old
and never left the Temple, serving God night and day with
fasting and prayer. • She came by just at that moment and
began to praise God; and she spoke of the child to all who
looked forward to the deliverance of Jerusalem.

    • When they had done everything the Law of the Lord
required, they went back to Galilee, to their own town of
Nazareth.

This is a "stained glass episode" . . . (45, p. 59), elaborate, rich, and trans-lucent, the climax of the events surrounding the birth of Jesus.

We have made the journey from the cave of Bethlehem to the Temple in Jerusalem, from the birthing cave to the temple of sacrifice.

Encapsulated within the complexities of the passage is the deep faith and ful-fillment experience of the primitive Christian community.

We are invited to contemplate a rich collage of Hebrew Scripture phrases, Jewish rituals, poetry, prophecy, and prayer. Spanning human experience, Luke portrays for us the newborn child, the young parental couple, the wise old man and woman.

Through Luke's deft artistry, we, too, enter the Temple experience and are brought to witness the public acknowledgement of Jesus' identity and destiny.

Yet, for all this complexity, Mary was still

A woman dusty for the six mile road
With a Child that pressed her warm beneath the shawls,
and a heart that wished no more than this. (Ibid)

Mary, obedient to the inner spirit of the Law, came with Jesus into the Tem-ple for the purpose of presenting her firstborn son to the Lord, as well as for the ritual purification required of all women after childbirth.

The practice of consecrating the firstborn son ritualized the Jewish belief that the first fruits of womb or field belonged to the service of God. It recalled the deliverance from Egypt when the firstborn of the Hebrews were spared (Exod. 13:11–16).

Mary, in communion with everyone who participated in birthing life, returned to the Temple, one of the "navels of the world" (55, p. 132). She who in submission had willingly entered into the containment of transformative birth now had come to the time of her emergence, signified by the cultic rituals of her purification (Lev. 12:1ff).

Mary will be identified, now, not only as the Virgin Mother of Christ, but as his first disciple.

There was in the Temple a man named Simeon grown old in God's service, known as one of "the quiet in the land" (5, p. 26). All his life he had waited patiently and quietly for God, for the comforting of Israel (Isa. 40:1ff).

Simeon received Jesus from the arms of Mary, and though an old man held the child, it was in reality the child who held the aged man.

More than a "watchman on the coming of dawn" (Ps. 130:6), Simeon recognized in the child the coming of the new day that Israel had so long expected. His wait over, the promise fulfilled, Simeon prayed joyfully, "Now, Master, you can let your servant go in peace. . . ."

In the ecstasy of letting go, Simeon assumed the role of the true prophet. He proclaimed the contradictions that would accompany the peace Christ brings. Jesus is the sword of discriminating judgment. Simeon presents us with the unrelenting, harsh reality that, ultimately, *we* must choose. Our pain, like Mary's pain, will be this burden of personal discernment and the realization that Christ will be rejected and that those we love may not stand beside us. There is no escaping—all that is hidden will come to light.

In Simeon's oracle, we are confronted with the wholeness of Christ. Looking into the eyes of the child Jesus, Simeon saw at once the shadow of death and the glory of creation renewed.

Anna joined Simeon in prophecy. The eloquence of Simeon's words was paralleled by the eloquence of the life of the aged woman with whom Luke closes this episode. Sustained in hope by prayer and fasting, her life was her prophecy.

The day *has* come. The Lord *has* entered his Temple. It is the Lord who speaks:

I will pour out my spirit on all [humankind],
Your sons and daughters shall prophesy,

your old men shall dream dreams,
and your young men see visions. (Joel 3:1; Acts 2:17)

Suggested Approach to Prayer: In the Temple

+ *Daily prayer pattern:* (See pages 1 and 2.)
I quiet myself and relax in the presence of God.
I declare my dependency on God.

+ *Grace:* I ask to know Jesus more intimately, to love him more intensely, to follow him more closely.

+ *Method:* Contemplation, as on page 3.
I am present within the Temple as Mary and Joseph present their son, Jesus, as an offering to God.
I envision in detail the interior of the Temple—the entrances, the walls, the pillars, the altars. I hear the sounds. . . . I am aware of the scents. . . .
I allow myself to be engaged in the unfolding event. I listen attentively to the words that are spoken. I see the expressions and the gestures of each person. I participate and respond in whatever manner emerges from within me.

+ *Closing:* I stay with Mary and offer joy, thanks, wonder, and praise. I beg for the grace to know and to draw close to Jesus.
I pray the Our Father.

+ *Review of Prayer:* I record in my journal the feelings and understandings that have come through the time of prayer.

Week II, Day 2: The Quest

MATTHEW 2:1–12

After Jesus had been born at Bethlehem in Judaea during the reign of King Herod, some wise men came to Jerusalem from the east. • "Where is the infant king of the jews?" they asked. "We saw his star as it rose and have come to do him homage." • When King Herod heard this, he was perturbed, and so was the whole of Jerusalem. • He called together all the chief priests and the scribes of the people, and enquired of them where the Christ was to be born. • "At Bethlehem in Judaea," they told him, "for this is what the prophet wrote:

And you, Bethlehem, in the land of Judah,
you are by no means least among the leaders of Judah,
for out of you will come a leader
who will shepherd my people Israel."

• Then Herod summoned the wise men to see him privately. He asked them the exact date on which the star had appeared, • and sent them on to Bethlehem. "Go and find out all about the child," he said, "and when you have found him, let me know, so that I too may go and do him homage." • Having listened to what the king had to say, they set out. And there in front of them was the star they had seen rising; it went forward and halted over the place where the child was. • The sight of the star filled them with delight, • and going into the house they saw the child with his mother Mary, and falling to their knees they did him homage. Then, opening their treasures, they offered him gifts of gold and frankincense and myrrh. • But they were warned in a dream not to go back to Herod, and returned to their own country by a different way.

"Star light, star bright, first star I see tonight. . . ."

Do you still recite this childhood poem of desire at the sight of the first evening star? Many people do; if not aloud, then within their childheart.

The poem holds something of the theme of the story of the Magi. The wise ones followed the star in search of their desire, the holy child.

The symbol of the star is intrinsic to all beginnings, to birth. Poets and physicists describe the incredible primordial stellar explosion of concentrated energy that spawned the cosmos. This magnetic energy continues to give and to order life. We are all a part of and share in this cosmogenic activity; the beginning is within each of us.

Irresistibly, as to the source of their being, men and women have always been drawn to the contemplation of the stars.

The Magi were in search of a new beginning. As members of a Persian priestly cast and as astrologers, they used their belief in that phenomenon of nature—the stars—to guide them in the quest for the newborn King whose birth had been foretold and long expected.

Nature alone, however, was not enough to bring them to their child king. Some acquaintance with the Hebrew prophecy prompted their journey to Jerusalem to seek further enlightenment.

Summoned by King Herod, they came face to face with official Judaism. Historically, Herod is remembered for the vicious murdering of members of his own family as well as of political rivals. Suspicious and threatened, he cloaked his evil intent toward the new King with the facade of solicitude.

Ironically, the enlightenment the Magi sought came to them out of the darkness of Herod's heart. Unwittingly, Herod became God's instrument in guiding the Magi to the new King.

While the religious practice of the Jews had succumbed to an empty formalism and apathy, it was the pagan Magi, the Gentiles, who were filled with enthusiasm by the Jewish prophecies.

After leaving Jerusalem, the Wise Men were delighted with the renewed appearance of their star. It led them to the Child with his mother.

Seeing the child, they believed. Having finally succeeded in their search, they fell on their knees in adoration before their King.

One day the title "king of the Jews," with which this newborn infant was acclaimed, would be written over his cross as the mocking sign of his rejection (Matt. 27:37).

Having discovered at last a king worthy of their lives, they opened their treasures and offered all they had.

These were the forerunners of the Gentile nations who would come to Christ (Matt. 28:19).

Faithful to their star, the Magi returned to their own country, renewed and alive in the treasure they had found in Jesus.

Suggested Approach to Prayer: Following the Star

+ *Daily prayer pattern:* (See pages 1 and 2.)
  I quiet myself and relax in the presence of God.
  I declare my dependency on God.

+ *Grace:* I ask to know Jesus more intimately, to love him more intensely, to follow him more closely.

+ *Method:* Contemplation, as on page 3.
  I place myself in imagination among the Magi as they travel from the rich green valleys of the east, through the desert and down through Palestine into Jerusalem. I am aware of the mysterious star that leads us.

  In Jerusalem, I, too, make inquiries of the people about where to find the newborn King.

  We continue to follow the star. I am aware of my inner feelings as we approach and enter the house in Bethlehem.

  I gaze on the mother and the child she holds. I realize that this is the one I have been seeking. Quietly, I adore him. I offer to him my greatest treasures.

+ *Closing:* I stay with Mary and Jesus and offer joy, thanks, wonder, and praise. I beg for the grace to know and to draw close to Jesus.
  I pray the Our Father.

+ *Review of Prayer:* I record in my journal my responses and offerings.

Week II, Day 3: Return from Egypt

MATTHEW 2:13–23

After they had left, the angel of the Lord appeared to Joseph in a dream and said, "Get up, take the child and his mother with you, and escape into Egypt, and stay there until I tell you, because Herod intends to search for the child and do away with him." • *So Joseph got up and, taking the child and his mother with him, left that night for Egypt,* • *where he stayed until Herod was dead. This was to fulfill what the Lord had spoken through the prophet:*

I called my son out of Egypt.

• *Herod was furious when he realised that he had been outwitted by the wise men, and in Bethlehem and its surrounding district he had all the male children killed who were two years old or under, reckoning by the date he had been careful to ask the wise men.* • *It was then that the words spoken through the prophet Jeremiah were fulfilled:*

A voice was heard in Ramah,
sobbing and loudly lamenting:
it was Rachel weeping for her children,
refusing to be comforted
because they were no more.

After Herod's death, the angel of the Lord appeared in a dream to Joseph in Egypt • *and said, "Get up, take the child and his mother with you and go back to the land of Israel, for those who wanted to kill the child are dead."* • *So Joseph got up and, taking the child and his mother with him, went back to the land of Israel.* • *But when he learnt that Archelaus had succeeded his father Herod as ruler of Judaea he was afraid to go there, and being warned in a dream he left for the region of*

Galilee. • *There he settled in a town called Nazareth. In this way the words spoken through the prophets were to be fulfilled:*

He will be called a Nazarene.

"The Flight into Egypt" is the traditional title given this passage. But "Return from Egypt" would more clearly speak to us of the underlying theme of God's plan of love. The passage focuses on *how* the fullness of God's promises is brought to realization.

In this threatening event of Jesus' early life, we are led to see how God is constantly and dynamically present in every detail that occurs within our lives. No event, however perverse and regardless of the evil intent that may precipitate it, is outside of God's plan.

Our God is

. . . a God who acts within the scope of human history, makes himself known in human happenings. . . . He is not a God . . . untouched by the world's suffering but one who actively takes part . . . in this somber history. He is . . . a sympathetic, compassionate God, in brief, *he is a God with a human face.* (43, p. 30)

This reality was concretely dramatized in the Exodus and the Exile, the two great events that served as the context for the writing of this episode in the life of Jesus, who is God become human.

The displacement of Jesus to Egypt and the subsequent homecoming to Nazareth recapitulated the remembered experience of his people.

In the rememberance of the Exodus, the Jewish people recalled how, under the leadership of Moses, they were, by God's merciful love, freed from the oppression of the Egyptian rulers and led through the Reed Sea to the promised land.

Likewise, in the Exile, they remembered the seventy years the people of Judah spent as refugees in the foreign city of Babylon and how God had provided for their release and homecoming through the mediation of the pagan king, Cyrus.

The human sufferings of these traumatic events were the two great tests which served as the vehicle through which Yahweh's faithful loving care was expressed and made visible.

Foreshadowing his future suffering and resurrection, Jesus, even as a child, was subjected to persecution. He, like the Israelites before him, was driven into the exile of Egypt. And just as God's loving kindness had formed and called forth Jesus' ancestors, so also was Jesus called forth.

"I called my son out of Egypt" (Hos. 11:1).

In applying to Jesus this passage from the Hebrew Scriptures, which originally referred to the entire Israelite community, Matthew subtly identified Jesus as the Son of God.

God's intervention in saving Jesus' life moved Herod to order the heinous murdering of all the male children in Bethlehem. This massacre recalls the earlier slaughter of the Hebrew children in Egypt by command of the Pharaoh (Exod. 1:15–21).

As if from the bowels of that grievous time, we hear again the weeping of Rachel, ancient mother of Israel. At her tomb in Ramah, those about to be sent into exile were gathered before their deportation.

Ingenuously Matthew has used this passage from Jeremiah to lead us to an experience of the power and presence of God-with-us (Matt. 1:23).

The words of Jeremiah dramatically arouse within us the remembrance of a pain so great that it, of necessity, plunges us to those profound recesses from which we are given the capacity to experience the measure of consolation that enables the surpassing and transforming of our reality.

This is the Jesus event!

The early Jewish Christian of Matthew's audience would have known of the consoling promise that followed Rachel's lament:

Stop your weeping,
dry your eyes,
your hardships will be redressed: . . . ·
your sons will come home to their own lands. . . .
I must still remember . . .
still be deeply moved . . .
let my tenderness yearn over him. . . .
Yahweh is creating something new on earth: . . . (Jer. 31:16,17,20,22).

Looking closely at this episode we are brought to the awareness that in the personal story of Jesus the central élan of the human story, as told in the Hebrew Scriptures, is healed and carried forward.

As a result, what may have been lost of the promise and potential of these historical ages may be found again and used in ways that would not have been possible . . . previously. (40, p. 30)

In Jesus, Son of God, the stories of the Hebrew Scriptures and our own stories are transcended and thereby transformed.

Suggested Approach to Prayer: With Joseph

+ *Daily prayer pattern:* (See pages 1 and 2.)
I quiet myself and relax in the presence of God.
I declare my dependency on God.

+ *Grace:* I ask to know Jesus more intimately, to love him more intensely, and to follow him more closely.

+ *Method:* Contemplation, as on page 3.
I place myself in the company of Joseph and listen attentively as he tells me about the dream warning him that Herod intended to destroy Jesus.

I listen as he relates the events of the long and arduous escape he made with Mary and the Child, through the desert.

He tells me of the homelessness they experienced in the foreign land of Egypt.

He shares with me the tremendous relief and joy that filled Mary and himself when they were able to return home in safety to Nazareth.

+ *Closing:* I stay with Mary and Jesus and offer joy, thanks, wonder, and praise. I beg for the grace to draw close to Jesus.
I pray the Our Father.

+ *Review of Prayer:* I record in my journal any feelings I experienced during this period of prayer, particularly those recalling memories of personal suffering which issued forth in new life.

Week II, Day 4: The Hidden Life

LUKE 2:51–52

He then went down with them and came to Nazareth and lived under their authority. His mother stored up all these things in her heart. • And Jesus increased in wisdom, in stature, and in favour with God and [people].

". . . and now the life you have is hidden with Christ in God" (Col. 3:3).

The "hidden life" is a common expression used to identify the years Jesus lived with Mary and Joseph in Nazareth. It speaks of those years of growth and development that formed and readied him for his adult ministry.

The Gospels give us only a brief glimpse of these formative years. What is conjectured is based on what can be gleaned from the Scriptures about his later life, as well as from what we know of the culture in which he lived.

Luke's brief words in 2:51–52 point to an ordinary childhood lived in obedience to Joseph and Mary. The gradual development of Jesus into a mature adult, spiritually, physically, and relationally, implies a home that was grounded in the wholesome balance of love, discipline, prayer, and work.

In our contemplation of these "hidden" years, we are led to seek out the underlying fundamental orientation that shaped his entire life and ministry.

Many of the images which have been absorbed by well-intentioned Christians have unfortunately proved to be inadequate and even detrimental to a balanced and authentic spiritual development. These images span the extremes from that of a "cardboard giant" to that of a sanguinely "sweet Jesus."

Regretfully, these representations have had the effect of distancing Jesus from our own human experience as well as removing us from the truth of *his* humanity.

For, Jesus was not only God; he *was* human. The human experience was his experience.

He, too, was delighted with being alive; he, too, was burdened with the pain of being alive. He struggled as we do with making a living, relating to people, controlling his emotions. He, also, loved to celebrate, to eat well, to enjoy his friends. No doubt he danced at Cana!

Jesus is not an abstraction. He is not an idea nor a theory, not a program nor a principle. He was an individual, historical, authoritative, concrete person.

The great gift that God gives us in Jesus is that we can see in another human being exactly what God has in mind for us. Jesus makes visible God's message. He shows us by the way he lived his life the basic attitude which we are to adopt in living our lives.

However, Jesus does not provide us with easy answers. In his person and in the events of his life—in his words, actions, sufferings, and joys—we are able to contemplate and translate into our own lives a basic orientation toward life. Within this—his—basic attitude, we can make decisions which not only advance our own humanness but that of the entire human community as well.

Hidden in the ordinary life of Jesus of Nazareth is the secret of where all ordinary life finds its ultimate meaning.

And we, with our unveiled faces reflecting like mirrors the brightness of the Lord, all grow brighter and brighter as we are turned into the image that we reflect; this is the work of the Lord who is Spirit. (2 Cor. 3:18)

Suggested Approach to Prayer: A Visit to Nazareth

+ *Daily prayer pattern:* (See pages 1 and 2.)
   I quiet myself and relax in the presence of God.
   I declare my dependency on God.

+ *Grace:* I ask to know Jesus more intimately, to love him more intensely and to follow him more closely.

+ *Method:* Contemplation, as on page 3.
   I enter into the home of Jesus at Nazareth, and spend time with Joseph and Mary and Jesus.
   I let emerge a day in their lives, letting Jesus be whatever age I am drawn to.
   I see the details of the little home . . . the furniture Joseph has made . . . Mary's kitchen . . . the shelf where Jesus keeps his belongings.
   I watch Jesus as he helps Joseph in the carpenter shop.

I smell Mary's afternoon baking.

I listen to the mealtime conversation and see the expressions on the faces of this family.

I watch and listen as Jesus interacts with his friends.

I continue in this manner, contemplating Jesus in the midst of his family.

+ *Closing:* I close my prayer by joining Jesus and Mary and Joseph in their evening prayer, adding my own offerings of joy, thanks, wonder, and praise.

I pray the Our Father.

+ *Review of Prayer:* I write in my journal any feelings or insights that emerged as I was present to Jesus' "hidden life."

Week II, Day 5: He Was Not Lost

LUKE 2:41–50

Every year his parents used to go to Jerusalem for the feast of the Passover. • When he was twelve years old, they went up for the feast as usual. • When they were on their way home after the feast, the boy Jesus stayed behind in Jerusalem without his parents knowing it. • They assumed he was with the caravan, and it was only after a day's journey that they went to look for him among their relations and acquaintances. • When they failed to find him they went back to Jerusalem looking for him everywhere.

• Three days later, they found him in the Temple, sitting among the doctors, listening to them, and asking them questions; • and all those who heard him were astounded at his intelligence and his replies. • They were overcome when they saw him, and his mother said to him, "My child, why have you done this to us? See how worried your father and I have been, looking for you." • "Why were you looking for me?" he replied, "Did you not know that I must be busy with my Father's affairs?" • But they did not understand what he meant.

For three days Joseph and Mary searched agonizingly for Jesus.
He was not lost!
"Why were you looking for me? . . . Did you not know that I must be busy with my Father's affairs?" These are the first words we hear Jesus speak. In this initial assertion, he claimed his own identity and mission.

Up to this time in the Gospels, others had clarified who he was, as when Simeon and Anna joyfully proclaimed him as the "long awaited one."

It would not have been unusual for a young man to remain behind in the Temple. As a festal celebration such as Passover drew to a close, the Sanhedrin conducted open forums. Jesus was probably one among many young men who were fascinated with the dialogue, asked questions, and expounded their own youthful wisdom. The "wisdom" of Jesus, however, apparently made an impression on his elders.

Evidently, Jesus had a sense of "being at home" in the Temple. Even at this early age, he exhibited an awareness of his unique relationship with God as Father and, flowing from that relationship, a vital conviction of mission. It is not incidental, then, that the Temple was the place where Jesus chose to initially declare his independence.

The youthful Jesus, seized with the dream of new possibilities, was filled with the energy of exploration, challenge, and creativity. The response to his mother's concern clearly indicated his decision to claim as his priority the fulfillment of his dream, God's will for him. It also indicated his willingness to accept the detachments that were essential for the emergence of his mission.

Are *we* lost? Have we found our way to the place where our God dwells?

The gift that Christ gives us in this passage is that he is so filled with being God's son, so committed, that we, too, "catch" the dream for our lives.

Jesus calls us to be faithful to our "extended self," that is, to live our lives so that the fullest measure of our potential will be actualized. Jesus showed us that the practical way to do this is through the discovery of our unique relationship with God and by committing our whole being to what emerges as our particular mission.

For us, as for Jesus, the living out of the new reality of *self in God* will demand some wrenching detachments. It will open us to being misunderstood even by those who are closest to us. It will plunge us into the very midst of life and will require of us constant prayer and courage.

Through those found in Christ, God speaks to the world. God will speak through our lives, conveying the same hope that was addressed to the Israelites in the words of Jeremiah:

I know the plans I have in mind for you—it is Yahweh who speaks—plans for peace, not disaster, reserving a future full of hope for you. . . . When you seek me you shall find me, when you seek me with all your heart. (Jer. 29:11,13)

Suggested Approach to Prayer: A Shared Dream

+ *Daily prayer pattern:* (See pages 1 and 2.)
I quiet myself and relax in the presence of God.
I declare my dependency on God.

+ *Grace:* I ask to know Jesus more intimately, to love him more intensely, and to follow him more closely.

+ *Method:* Contemplation, as on page 3.
With Mary and Joseph, I search for the young Jesus. I am aware of their anxious concern.

I see their relief upon finding him in the Temple.

I see all the details of the scene in the Temple. I see the Temple itself and his expressions of amazement on the faces of the elders.

I watch as Mary approaches and questions Jesus. I am particularly aware of Jesus' response. I am aware of how his conviction is expressed in his words, in the emotional tone, in his physical stance.

I allow myself to absorb the love, encouragement, and empowerment that fills him.

+ *Closing:* I share with Mary, Jesus, and God, my Creator, the deep desire and dreams I have to be all that God wants me to be. I thank Christ for the direction his life gives me. I share with him my need for courage.

I close my prayer by slowly reciting the Our Father, as if I have just heard it for the first time.

+ *Review of Prayer:* I record in my journal the dreams and desires that may have emerged in the prayer period and any feelings that accompanied them.

Week II, Day 6: Repetition

Suggested Approach to Prayer

+ *Daily prayer pattern:* (See pages 1 and 2.)
I quiet myself and relax in the presence of God.
I declare my dependency on God.

+ *Grace:* I ask to know Jesus more intimately, to love him more intensely, and to follow him more closely.

+ *Method:* Repetition, as on page 6.
In preparation, I review my previous prayer periods by reading my journal since the last repetition day. I select for my repetiton the period of prayer in which I was most deeply moved, or the one in which I experienced a lack of emotional response. I use the method with which I approached the passage initially. I open myself to hear again God's word to me in that particular passage.

+ *Review of Prayer:* I write in my journal any feelings, experiences, or insights that have surfaced in this "second listening."

Before Proceeding

Dear Friend in Christ,

The kingdom of God *has* come! The kingdom of God is among us! (Luke 17:21).

Each of us has a unique experience of the presence of the Kingdom in our midst. Within our daily lives, we have quiet moments of healing, peace, and knowing, moments of joy and realization.

The larger world, too, manifests a presence of the Kingdom. The Spirit of the Risen Lord is particularly evident in the upsurge of interest in and commitment to spiritual renewal which is taking place in all faiths. The Kingdom is made visible in those movements which advance global consciousness and global responsibility. There are myriad ways in which individuals and societies are attempting to become more aware of and more caring for the human family and its cosmic home.

The evolutionary process of the Kingdom of God is well under way!

The Kingdom of God is within us. When Christ appears in the clouds, he will simply be manifesting a metamorphosis that has been slowly accomplished under his influence in the heart of the mass of humankind. (69, p. 128)

As Christians we believe in and draw strength from the presence of the Kingdom growing within and among us.

We are, at the same time, in touch with the blatant reality of an evil force which is counter to the growth of the Kingdom. Granted, it is not equal to the force of good, but nonetheless it is a pervasive presence which is like weeds among the wheat.

Unfortunately, some weeds are less easy to spot than others, yet they wield a no less destructive force. They, too, choke out life. Frequently, we fail to recognize the power of evil in its subtle seductiveness. To recognize the more insidious forms of evil requires an astute sensitivity and the courage to examine our innermost selves.

We must look within our hearts to discover where we are most fearful and insecure, for in these areas of our vulnerability we will most easily be ensnared.

The process of entrapment sneaks up on us. Usually the first enticement is something we desire to possess. This is not limited to material things. It is, however, closely related to a desire for approval, acceptance, and praise. These basic desires feed on each other and provide their own momentum.

The process spirals: Look at what I have . . . look at me . . . look at who I am.

Under the guise of "getting ahead" and providing for the future, we can easily move into a state of apathy in regard to evil and in many instances to a denial of its existence.

As followers of Christ we are not exempt from the enticements of the evil one. "Your enemy the devil is prowling round like a roaring lion, looking for someone to eat" (1 Pet. 5:8).

The writings of Vatican II remind us

Man . . . is divided in himself. As a result, the whole life of people, both individual and social, shows itself to be a struggle, and a dramatic one, between good and evil, between light and darkness. People find that they are unable of themselves to overcome the assaults of evil successfully, so that everyone feels as though bound by chains. But the Lord himself came to free and strengthen his people, renewing them inwardly and casting out the "prince of this world" (John 12:31), who held him in the bondage of sin. (1, Church in the Modern World, Par. 13)

With Christ, Christians are to face the challenge of the struggle against evil and thereby to participate in the actualization of the Kingdom of God.

In the commentaries and approaches of the following days, you will enter into a reflective process to discover how you are personally being called to advance the Kingdom of God. It is important to allow yourself sufficient time and space for discernment. For example, you may need to spend several periods of prayer on any one particular exercise or "day."

These contemplations, known in Ignatian Spirituality as the Two Standards, will lead you through vivid imagery to a growing sensitivity of the strategies of the evil one. You will also be led to a deepening appreciation for Jesus and the way he draws you to service in the Kingdom.

"Glory to Him who is able to give you the strength to live according to the Good News. . . ." (Rom. 16:25).

Week III, Day 1: Focus on Jesus

1 TIMOTHY 6:3–12

This is what you are to teach them to believe and persuade them to do. Anyone who teaches anything different, and does not keep to the sound teaching which is that of our Lord Jesus Christ, the doctrine which is in accordance with true religion, • is simply ignorant and must be full of self-conceit—with a craze for questioning everything and arguing about words. All that can come of this is jealousy, contention, abuse and wicked mistrust of one another; • and unending disputes by people who are neither rational nor informed and imagine that religion is a way of making a profit. • Religion, of course, does bring large profits, but only to those who are content with what they have. • We brought nothing into the world, and we can take nothing out of it; • but as long as we have food and clothing, let us be content with that. • People who long to be rich are a prey to temptation; they get trapped into all sorts of foolish and dangerous ambitions which eventually plunge them into ruin and destruction. • The love of money is the root of all evils and there are some who, pursuing it, have wandered away from the faith, and so given their souls any number of fatal wounds.

But, as a [person] dedicated to God, you must avoid all that. You must aim to be saintly and religious, filled with faith and love, patient and gentle. • Fight the good fight of the faith and win for yourself the eternal life to which you were called when you made your profession and spoke up for the truth in front of many witnesses.

In his concern for his protege, Timothy, Paul set out to refute the false religious teachings current in his time. His primary motive was to encourage and strengthen Timothy, "a man dedicated to God" and actively engaged in ministry.

Paul cautioned Timothy about the importance of staying true to Christ.

He was made visible in the flesh,
attested by the Spirit,
seen by angels,
proclaimed to the pagans,
believed in by the world,
taken up in glory. (1 Tim. 3:16)

During the early development of the Church, an upsurge of zealous "evangelists" arose who were eager to promote religion for their own profit. Their teachings were superficial and preyed on the vulnerabilities of the insecure.

Paul was very concerned about the distortions of the Gospel that subtly denied the reality of the human experience of Jesus and therefore negated the goodness of creation.

The mystery of the person of Christ is profound.

The false teaching, which emphasized knowledge and elitism, squelched the hope of the young Christian community and robbed it of its joy. As a result, the people were filled with self-doubt and were left feeling neither smart enough nor good enough.

Paul warned Timothy that in their disillusionment, the people were in danger of being swept into all kinds of self-satisfying seductions. He was intent that they maintain a proper attitude and balance, particularly in regard to the riches and honors of this world.

Certainly Paul did not want the members of the young community to be subject to the miseries of poverty or ridicule. His deep desire was that their allegiance be to God and to the creative action that had begun within them.

"You must love the Lord your God with all your heart, with all your soul, and with all your mind (Matt. 22:37). This alone would make the church "God's family" (1 Tim. 3:15).

Paul was telling Timothy—and us—to keep our eyes focused on Jesus, and then, wherever we go, God will be there ahead of us.

With the confidence that this direction inspires, we will not then lose sight of the reality that God calls us most deeply to faithfulness within the events and circumstances of ordinary daily life.

The humanity of Jesus demands of us a radical grounding in our own humanity. Centered in Jesus and grounded in life, we become receptive to the gestation of Christ's life within us (Gal. 4:19).

Strengthened interiorly by the gradual unfolding of new life within and continually drawn by the magnetic attraction of Christ, we are enabled to discern our paths through the distractions and temptations that surround us. We are given a measure of freedom from the compulsive, addictive behaviors that are a part of every human struggle.

Our compulsiveness is replaced by compassion. Joy is discovered, not in the gathering of things, the attainment of praises, or the exaggerations of self; it is found, rather, in the extension of ourselves in loving and caring relationships with others.

Suggested Approach to Prayer: From Riches to Freedom

+ *Daily prayer pattern:* (See pages 1 and 2.)
    I quiet myself and relax in the presence of God.
    I declare my dependency on God.

+ *Method:* Contemplation, as on page 3 and Meditation, as on page 3.
    I see before me, at opposite poles, Christ and Satan. I hear Christ call my name and invite me to join him. I see Satan entice me to his side.
    I see two places.
    I see Jerusalem, city of peace, representing the Kingdom of God. In it, the followers of Christ are gathering around their Lord, Jesus.
    I see Babylon, city of evil, representing the region of Satan. Those who have chosen to follow Satan are gathered around Satan, their chief.

+ *Grace:* I ask for what I want.
    I ask for the knowledge to be able to detect the strategies of Satan. I beg for help against the particular tactics of evil to which I am most vulnerable.
    I ask for the knowledge of true life in Christ in order that I will be able to follow the pattern of Christ's life and make all my decisions in light of his way.

+ *Approach—Part 1:*

I see Satan sitting on his throne in the center of the city of Babylon. He is surrounded by fire and smoke. I imagine his contriving looks. I see him snarl as he issues demands to his underlings. He sends out these demons, disguised, throughout the whole world to every country, every town, to every home, and to each individual.

I hear Satan instruct the demons to put out their nets and be ready to chain those they tempt. Satan tells them the first temptation they are to cast out is a *longing for riches.*

+ *Approach—Part 2:*

I see Christ as he is within the city of peace. I image the beauty of this place, the quiet gentleness of undisturbed nature. I see Christ sitting among his followers. He is gently inviting them to participate in his ministry of love. He sends them, as his disciples, to all the people of the world. His love extends through his followers to all persons regardless of their circumstances or their situation in life.

I see that Christ's way is the opposite of Satan's. Instead of chaining people, Jesus wishes to free his people from whatever would bind and hinder them from being totally open to life. He calls them to nurture within themselves a poverty of spirit, that is, a total dependency on God, and a balanced attitude toward the things and the honors of this world. Christ may even call some of his followers to witness to this inner freedom through physical poverty.

+ *Reflection:*

"People who long to be rich are a prey to temptation; they get trapped into all sorts of foolish and dangerous ambitions which eventually plunge them into ruin and destruction."

Considering that some of the key tools Satan uses are fear, exaggeration, self-pity, self-doubt, and discouragement, I reflect on questions like the following to become more aware of his strategy and how he effects it in my life:

- How does fear of the unknown lead me to compulsively seek wealth and status?

- How does self-pity lead me to destructive negative thinking and denial of my talents and/or those of others?
- How does exaggeration lead me to lying and bragging?
- How does self-doubt keep me from developing and exercising my talents of intellect, of will, of heart and body?
- How does a sense of discouragement lead me to under-achieving?
- On a global level, how do I see people being controlled by these same evil tools in overconsumerism, for example, or the imbalance of wealth?

"You must . . . be . . . filled with faith and love, patient and gentle."

Considering that Christ's approach is characterized by honesty, gratefulness, receptivity, and genuineness, I reflect on questions like the following to better grasp the approach of Jesus and to be open to his influence in my life:
- How does the experience of gratitude for the gifts of the earth and for my talents free me from possessiveness and release me to share with others?
- How does openness free me to acclaim the gifts of others?
- How does being honest release me from even subtly cheating others of their due wages or recognition of basic needs? How does being honest release me from inflation of self or from expecting too much of myself?
- How does genuineness free me from overstriving so that I may live in a spirit of contentment with what I have?
- On a global scale, how do I see nations and peoples being freed by embracing Christ's standard, for example, through ecology concerns, programs to relieve hunger, and the like?

+ *Closing:* I ask Mary to intercede for me that I would receive the gift of total dependency on God. I ask that I would be so detached from all things that I would put all my talents, possessions, and achievements at the service of Christ. I pray to follow in the pattern of Christ's life—even to the end. Providing it would not be sinful on anyone's part, I pray that if it is God's wish for me, I would have, like Christ, the courage and strength to endure poverty and/or personal humiliation.

I pray the Hail Mary.

In the company of Mary, I approach Jesus and offer the same prayer that he would obtain these graces for me from my Creator. I pray "Soul of Christ," p. 141.

In the presence of Jesus and Mary, and offered by them, I approach God my Creator. Again I make the same request.

I pray the Our Father.

+ *Review of Prayer:* I record in my journal any new awareness I have of how the devil works in my life, as well as any new appreciation I have for the way Jesus draws me into his life. I record any accompanying feelings.

Week III, Day 2: Guided By the Spirit

GALATIANS 5:16–25

Let me put it like this: if you are guided by the Spirit you will be in no danger of yielding to self-indulgence, • since self-indulgence is the opposite of the Spirit, the Spirit is totally against such a thing, and it is precisely because the two are so opposed that you do not always carry out your good intentions. • If you are led by the Spirit, no law can touch you. • When self-indulgence is at work, the results are obvious: fornication, gross indecency and sexual irresponsibility; idolatry and sorcery; feuds and wrangling, jealousy, bad temper and quarrels; disagreements, factions, • envy; drunkenness, orgies and similar things. I warn you now, as I warned you before: those who behave like this will not inherit the kingdom of God. • What the Spirit brings is very different: love, joy, peace, patience, kindness, goodness, trustfulness, • gentleness and self-control. There can be no law against things like that, of course. • You cannot belong to Christ Jesus unless you crucify all self-indulgent passions and desires.

Since the Spirit is our life, let us be directed by the Spirit.

There is within each of us an "angel of goodness." We know that "angel" as our innermost, basic tendency toward good, toward God. The "angel of goodness" is that within us which counsels and encourages us toward our most authentic response and decision.

We can also identify an "angel of darkness" within our souls. This dark "angel" is perceived as the conflictual drive toward fragmentation and destruction.

We are not angels! We are human beings caught in the valiant task of wrestling with the seemingly more-than-human, opposing forces within us.

We are not, however, alone in this conflict. Christ is active within us with the power of his Spirit. It is precisely within this struggle that the Spirit empowers us to wholeness. We can be encouraged by keeping in mind always that the force of good outweighs the force of evil.

In his letter to the Galatians, Paul names these two forces within as spirit and flesh. By spirit he means the cooperation of our deepest selves with the spirit of God. In referring to flesh, Paul does not imply any negative connotation regarding the body, but rather uses it as the symbol of all within us which opposes goodness.

The challenge is to be guided by the Spirit, discerning the signs along the way. These signs are made evident within the human experience of our daily lives.

To the small Christian community in Galatia, Paul writes his reassurance, "if you are guided by the spirit you will be in no danger of yielding to self-indulgence."

The two lists—of vices and virtues—that Paul presents, illustrate that "there where clinging to things ends, God begins to be" (33, p. 160).

Penetrated by the Spirit of God, our lives become fruitful. Birth happens in the grace of letting go.

The Spirit's own gift of patience awakens within us a sensitivity and receptivity to the process of our own inner healing. In the letting go of useless shame and false guilt, a space for new possibilities is born. By enabling us to embrace a gentle discipline, the spirit of freedom brings balance and harmony. The spirit further encourages us to dare to expose our vulnerability and to trust ourselves to loving and being loved by others. The fruit of the Spirit becomes evident in the gentle attentiveness to allowing others to be who they are. Above all, the Spirit rejoices in our laughter and enjoyment in a world filled with the energy and beauty of ongoing creation.

Paul exemplified the practice of letting go.

Patterned on the life of Jesus, Paul's life was one of total surrender to the spirit within him. His life was completely given over to preaching the power of the Spirit and transformation in Christ. He was never discouraged by the new Christians' lack of understanding, nor by their rigid adherence to the formalities of the law. Paul simply continued always to urge the Christians of Galatia to embrace for themselves the Christ who gave him ultimate meaning and joy.

His words encapsulate his deep identification with and commitment to Christ, "I live now not with my own life but with the life of Christ who lives in me" (Gal. 2:20).

Suggested Approach to Prayer: From Honors to Vulnerability

+ *Daily prayer pattern:* (See pages 1 and 2.)
I quiet myself and relax in the presence of God.
I declare my dependency on God.

+ *Method:* Contemplation, as on page 3 and Meditation, as on page 3.
I see before me, at opposite poles, Christ and Satan. I hear Christ call my name and invite me to join him. I see Satan entice me to his side.
I see two places.
I see Jerusalem, city of peace, representing the Kingdom of God. In it, the followers of Christ are gathering around their Lord, Jesus.
I see Babylon, city of evil, representing the region of Satan. Those who have chosen to follow Satan are gathered around Satan, their chief.

+ *Grace:* I ask for what I want.
I ask for the knowledge to be able to detect the strategies of Satan. I beg for help against the particular tactics of evil to which I am most vulnerable.
I ask for the knowledge of true life in Christ in order that I will be able to follow the pattern of Christ's life and make all my decisions in light of his way.

+ *Approach—Part 1:*
I see Satan sitting on his throne in the center of the city of Babylon. He is surrounded by fire and smoke. I imagine how he looks. I see the snarl and his contriving looks as he issues demands to his underlings. He sends out these demons, disguised, throughout the whole world to every country, every town, to every home, and to each individual.
I hear Satan instruct the demons to put out their nets and be ready to chain those they tempt. Satan tells them the second temptation they are to cast out is a *longing for honors and esteem.*

+ *Approach—Part 2:*
I see Christ as he is within the city of peace. I image the beauty of this place, the quiet gentleness of undisturbed nature. I see Christ sitting among his followers. He is gently inviting them to participate in his ministry of love. He

sends them, as his disciples, to all the people of the world. His love extends through his followers to all persons regardless of their circumstances or their situation in life.

I see that Christ's way is the opposite of Satan's. Instead of chaining people, Jesus wishes to free his people from whatever would bind them and hinder them from being totally open to life. He calls them to nurture within themselves a poverty of spirit, that is, a total dependency on God, and a balanced attitude toward the things and the honors of this world. Christ may even call some of his followers to witness to this inner freedom through physical poverty and personal humiliation.

+ *Reflection:*
"When self-indulgence is at work, the results are obvious. . . ."
Reflecting on some of the tools Satan uses, such as fear, exaggeration, self-pity, self-doubt, and discouragement, I consider questions like the following to become more aware of his strategy and how he effects it in my life:

- How does fear erode my trust of others and of myself?
- How does fear cause me to wear a mask that hides my true feelings, my weaknesses, and even my strength from others?
- How does fear drive me to secure my position and status at any expense to self or others?
- How does my exaggeration or understatement of self act to manipulate people into praising me?
- How does exaggeration cause me to over-evaluate myself and, consequently, to demand unjust recognition or recompense?
- How does self-doubt push me to be pompous, that is, to be "front and center"?
- How does self-doubt addict me to an insatiable appetite for perfection and affirmation?
- On a global level, how do I see people being controlled by these same evil tools through hero worship of "stars," for example, or the building of weapons of destruction, or rampant nationalism?

"What the spirit brings is very different: love, joy, peace, patience, kindness, goodness, trustfulness, gentleness and self-control."

Considering that Christ's approach is characterized by honesty, gratefulness, receptivity, and genuineness, I reflect on questions like the following to better grasp the approach of Jesus and to be open to his influence in my life:

- How does gratefulness allow me to celebrate the achievements of self and others?
- How does honesty free me to recognize my own limitations and to welcome constructive criticism from others?
- How does being receptive open me to mutually trusting and transparent relationships?
- How does openness release courage within me to dare to risk failure and rejection?
- How does genuineness release me from empty formalism and aloofness?
- On a global scale, how do I see nations and people being freed for life-giving potential by embracing the standard of Christ?

+ *Closing:* I ask Mary to intercede for me that I would receive the gift of total dependency on God. I ask that I would be so detached from all things that I would put all my talents, possessions, and achievements at the service of Christ. I pray to follow in the pattern of Christ's life—even to the end. Providing it would not be sinful on anyone's part, I pray that if it is God's wish for me, I would have, like Christ, the courage and strength to endure poverty and/or personal humiliation.

I pray the Hail Mary.

In the company of Mary, I approach Jesus and offer the same prayer, that he would obtain these graces for me from my Creator. I pray "Soul of Christ," p. 141.

In the presence of Jesus and Mary, and offered by them, I approach God my Creator. Again I make the same request.

I pray the Our Father.

+ *Review of Prayer:* I record in my journal any new awareness I have of how the devil works in my life, as well as any new appreciation I have for the way Jesus draws me into his life. I record any accompanying feelings.

Week III, Day 3: From Me to Us

MARK 10:35-45

*James and John, the sons of Zebedee, approached him.
"Master," they said to him, "we want you to do us a favour." •
He said to them, "What is it you want me to do for you?" •
They said to him, "Allow us to sit one at your right hand and
the other at your left in your glory." • "You do not know what
you are asking," Jesus said to them. "Can you drink the cup
that I must drink, or be baptised with the baptism with which I
must be baptised?" • They replied, "We can." Jesus said to
them, "The cup that I must drink you shall drink, and with the
baptism with which I must be baptised you shall be baptised, •
but as for seats at my right hand or my left, these are not mine
to grant; they belong to those to whom they have been allotted."*

*• When the other ten heard this they began to feel indig-
nant with James and John, • so Jesus called them to him and
said to them, "You know that among the pagans their so-called
rulers lord it over them, and their great men make their authority felt. This is not to happen among you. No; anyone who
wants to become great among you must be your servant, • and
anyone who wants to be first among you must be slave to all. •
For the Son of Man himself did not come to be served but to
serve, and to give his life as a ransom for many."*

The journey from "me" to "us" is a long one. True community totally upsets
the established "pecking order" in every area of life—political, religious, economic,
familial. The big question always is, Who is best . . . Who is first?

Poor James and John. They, too, were trapped in the game of wanting to
win. Mark shows us that the disciples were very slow in comprehending the
message of Jesus. They continued to arrogantly pursue the wrong question. They
continued to ask, "Who is the greatest?" (Mark 9:34), while the real questions
were "Who is Jesus?" and "Who are we?"

Jesus' reply to the two disciples seemed evasive. "Do you know what you are asking? Are you really willing to pattern your life after mine? Are you able to accept the sufferings of *your* life? Are you able to drink with me this common cup?"

If they were to refuse or to deny suffering, they would refuse life.

Once again, Jesus set before them the authentic way to greatness. The ultimate meaning of life would be experienced in the active endurance and integration of the ordinary disappointments, failures, and losses that are a part of living.

The game of one-upmanship had come to an abrupt halt.

It had, however, aroused anger on the part of the other disciples toward James and John. It was as if they had asked, "So what happens to us?"

The game of "greatness" is the game of rivalry. If there is a first, there is a second and a third and, ultimately, a last. The game is that destructive.

Jesus used the occasion of this foolish yet painful episode to instruct his disciples on the further implication of this radical reversal of values.

Greatness would be measured not by the domination or control of others but by the extension of themselves in service to others.

Jesus was especially firm in his demand that those among his followers who were in leadership were not to elevate themselves with a display of pomp and authority. They, particularly, were to exemplify his own submission in service.

The service that Jesus rendered and to which he called his disciples was not motivated by bargaining; he did not give with one hand and clutch with the other. Jesus voluntarily extended himself to others, motivated solely by his love for them. Only an act of pure love has the power to bring others out of a sinful pattern of life. It is only through love like this that we are transformed. Through the service of unconditional loving, we, too, are empowered to participate in the transformation of others.

The journey from "me" to "us" is, indeed, a journey of trust—of trust in God, in others, and in our deepest selves.

Suggested Approach to Prayer: From Pride to Unconditional Love

+ *Daily prayer pattern:* (See pages 1 and 2.)
  I quiet myself and relax in the presence of God.
  I declare my dependency on God.

+ *Method:* Contemplation, as on page 3 and Meditation, as on page 3.

I see before me, at opposite poles, Christ and Satan. I hear Christ call my name and invite me to join him. I see Satan entice me to his side.

I see two places.

I see Jerusalem, city of peace, representing the Kingdom of God. In it, the followers of Christ are gathering around their Lord, Jesus.

I see Babylon, city of evil, representing the region of Satan. Those who have chosen to follow Satan are gathered around Satan, their chief.

+ *Grace:* I ask for what I want.

I ask for the knowledge to be able to detect the strategies of Satan. I beg for help against the particular tactics of evil to which I am most vulnerable.

I ask for the knowledge of true life in Christ in order that I will be able to follow the pattern of Christ's life and make all my decisions in light of his way.

+ *Approach—Part 1:*

I see Satan sitting on his throne in the center of the city of Babylon. He is surrounded by fire and smoke. I imagine how he looks. I see his snarl and his contriving looks as he issues demands to his underlings. He sends out these demons, disguised, throughout the whole world to every country, every town, to every home, and to each individual.

I hear Satan instruct the demons to put out their nets and be ready to chain those they tempt. Satan tells them the third temptation they are to cast out is *pride*.

+ *Approach—Part 2:*

I see Christ as he is within the city of peace. I image the beauty of this place, the quiet gentleness of undisturbed nature. I see Christ sitting among his followers. He is gently inviting them to participate in his ministry of love. He sends them, as his disciples, to all the people of the world. His love extends through his followers to all persons regardless of their circumstances or their situation in life.

I see that Christ's way is the opposite of Satan's. Instead of chaining people, Jesus wishes to free his people from whatever would bind them and hinder them from being totally open to life. He calls them to nurture within themselves a poverty of spirit, that is, a total dependency on God, and a balanced attitude toward the things and the honors of this world. Christ may even call some of his followers to witness to this inner freedom through physical poverty and personal humiliation.

+ *Reflection:*

"You know that among the pagans their so-called rulers lord it over them, and their great men make their authority felt."

Considering that some of the key tools that Satan uses are fear, exaggeration, self-pity, self-doubt, and discouragement, I reflect on questions like the following to better discover his strategy and how he effects it in my life:

- How does fear of being dependent on others and lacking trust lead me to subtle and not so subtle forms of disordered self-sufficiency?
- How does exaggeration of self propel me into foolish games of "one-upmanship"?
- How does self-doubt drive me to be critical and demanding of others?
- How does a little authority and recognition puff me up and subject me to the whims of those I want to impress?
- How does discouragement devastate me and cause me to abandon hope?
- How does exaggerated self-importance turn a work of service or a deed of goodness into a self-centered, self-serving project?
- How does self-pity prompt me to attempt to do everything myself while whining all the time?
- How does exaggeration give me permission to use my role or position to seek special favors or privileges?
- On a global scale, how do I see people being controlled and crippled by these same evil strategies in, for example, the arms race?

"Anyone who wants to become great among you must be your servant."

Considering that Christ's approach is characterized by honesty, gratefulness, receptivity and genuineness, I reflect on questions like the following to better grasp the approach of Jesus and to be open to his influence in my life:

- How does gratitude for God's forgiving love of me open my heart to forgiving others?

- How does honesty demand of me an authentic non-judgmental response to others?
- How does the genuineness of Christ's love and service to others empower me to serve without reward and to suffer without retaliation?
- How does honesty lead me to embrace the reality that everyone, regardless of position, nationality, and the like, is my sister and brother?
- How does Christ's receptive willingness to suffer humiliation and contempt inspire me with the desire to unite my sufferings with his for the healing of the world?
- On a global scale, where do I see Christ's standard of humble, unconditional love being lived out today in, for example, the care and ministry to the needy, the unfortunate, the lost and confused, in the peace movement and efforts toward disarmament, by the missionaries in foreign lands?

+ *Closing:* I ask Mary to intercede for me that I would receive the gift of total dependency on God. I ask that I would be so detached from all things that I would put all my talents, possessions, and achievements at the service of Christ. I pray to follow in the pattern of Christ's life—even to the end. Providing it would not be sinful on anyone's part, I pray that if it is God's wish for me, I would have, like Christ, the courage and strength to endure poverty and/or personal humiliation.

I pray the Hail Mary.

In the company of Mary, I approach Jesus and offer the same prayer, that he would obtain these graces for me from my Creator. I pray "Soul of Christ," p. 141.

In the presence of Jesus and Mary, and offered by them, I approach God my Creator. Again I make the same request.

I pray the Our Father.

+ *Review of Prayer:* I record in my journal any new awareness I have of how the devil works in my life, as well as any new appreciation I have for the way Jesus draws me into his life. I record any accompanying feelings.

Week III, Day 4: Repetition

Suggested Approach to Prayer

+ *Daily prayer pattern:* (See pages 1 and 2.)
 I quiet myself and relax in the presence of God.
 I declare my dependency on God.

+ *Method:* Repetition, as on page 6.
 In preparation, I review my three previous prayer periods by reading my journal since the last repetition day. I select for my repetition the period of prayer in which I was most deeply moved, or the one in which I experienced spiritual aridity, that is, a lack of emotional response. I use the method with which I approached the passage initially. I open myself to hear again God's word to me in that particular passage.

+ *Grace:* I ask for the knowledge to be able to detect the strategies of Satan. I beg for help against the particular tactics of evil to which I am most vulnerable.
 I ask for the knowledge of true life in Christ in order that I will be able to follow the pattern of Christ's life and make all my decisions in light of his way.

+ *Review of Prayer:* I write in my journal any feelings, experiences, or insights that have surfaced in this "second listening."

Week III, Day 5: Three Persons

MATTHEW 6:33

Set your hearts on his kingdom first. . . .

Six hundred years ago, Saint Ignatius told the following story to those who came to him to share the struggle of their spiritual journey.

Once there were three people, each of whom received an unexpected, large sum of money. They were all very good people intent on serving God as best they could.

Who wouldn't have been excited?

After their initial exhilaration, the three, knowing the enormous responsibility entailed with the acquisition of such riches, became fearful.

All three asked, "What will this money do to me? How will my relationship with God be affected?"

Though the question for each was the same, their responses differed dramatically.

The first person became enamored with the money; he loved being wealthy! He enjoyed the prestige and security wealth brought to him. He handled his business affairs with the utmost integrity and secured the respect of all.

At the same time, he was aware of the effects the attachment was having on him. As he put his money in those investments which were the most profitable, he became progressively preoccupied with the returns he received. In his heart, he knew things were amiss. His conscience told him that there was more to life than this present comfortable existence. He told himself that someday, somehow, he would come to terms with this nagging voice within.

The "someday" never came. Without ever realizing what his inner voice was inviting him to enjoy, the man died.

The second person also became fascinated with her newly acquired wealth. However, almost from the beginning, she had a keen awareness of the ramifications of such wealth. She was especially concerned that her attachment not prove to be detrimental to her relationship with God. She found herself to be in the midst of a dilemma. On the one hand, she wanted to be free of her infatuation with the money, and on the other hand, she certainly did not want to lose control over this unexpected, fantastic windfall.

She reached the decision that it would please God if she were to do something truly wonderful for others with the money. So she determined to use a percentage of the interest the money earned to build a new library for the community in which she lived.

The building was impressive; on a cornerstone was inscribed not only the date, but her name as principal benefactor.

The third person, too, was immersed in concern and questioning upon receiving the large amount of money. His response was, "How can I best use this gift to reflect the pure goodness of God?" His approach was rooted in his deep conviction that God is the giver of all things. The man wanted only to do with the money what God wanted him to do.

Though he had no idea of what he should specifically do, he was confident that God would show him the way. So, at peace with this assurance, he secured the money in a trust fund to be used at the time the direction would be clear.

At the same time, he made a firm promise to nurture within himself an openness to God through prayer and to develop a sensitivity to the needs of others who might benefit by the trust fund.

Suggested Approach to Prayer: All Is Gift

+ *Daily prayer pattern:* (See pages 1 and 2.)
  I quiet myself and relax in the presence of God.
  I declare my dependency on God.

+ *Method:* Meditation as on page 3.
  I familiarize myself with the story.
  I see myself standing before God and all the saints. I take special note of the saints that have most inspired me.

As I stand alone before God and these saints, I beg for the grace to be free enough to choose from within God's particular call to me, what will *most* clearly radiate and make visible God's goodness in our world.

I focus my attention on the story. I see each of the three persons and image them in detail. I let surface whatever details my imagination releases, for example, what they look like, how old they are, their family situations, the daily circumstances of their lives.

In succession, I carefully consider the varied responses each has made.

I allow myself to take the place of each of the three persons. In the context of each of their responses, I consider the following questions:

- What are the gifts or "riches" that have been given to me?
- How are my responses similar or dissimilar to those of the first person. the second person? the third person?

In an attempt to become more aware of the disordered attachments that exist in my life and which are an obstacle to my total surrender to God, I consider questions like the following:

- What do my fears concerning loss tell me about what I cling to? (For example, loss of status, reputation, some particular possession.)
- Where in my life do I most frequently hear my voice of conscience . . . affirming . . . prodding . . . nagging me?
- What are those things which, good in themselves, tend to enslave me because of my attitude toward them? (For example, money, honors, work.)
- Have I responded possessively in my relationships with others, treating them as "things"?
- Where do I most experience the peace and freedom of being so totally attached to Christ that I can "take or leave" any particular thing, advantage, or honor?

Note: Becoming aware of the obstacles to one's responsive relationship to God frequently takes a long time and is very difficult. Once we make this discovery, however, Ignatius suggests that we take to prayer the very thing to which we are overly attached and ask that God remove it from us *if* it is truly God's will that we do not have that particular form of "riches." Ignatius encourages this radical and painful prayer as a means of transforming one's attitude from the consideration of the "riches" as "mine" to the realization that all is *gift* from God.

+ *Closing:* I ask Mary to intercede for me that I would receive the gift of total dependency on God. I ask that I would be so detached from all things that I would put all my talents, possessions, and achievements at the service of Christ. I pray to follow in the pattern of Christ's life—even to the end. Providing it would not be sinful on anyone's part, I pray that if it is God's wish for me, I would have, like Christ, the courage and strength to endure poverty and/or personal humiliation.

I pray the Hail Mary.

In the company of Mary, I approach Jesus and offer the same prayer, that he would obtain these graces for me from my Creator. I pray "Soul of Christ," p. 141.

In the presence of Jesus and Mary, and offered by them, I approach God my Creator. Again I make the same request.

I pray the Our Father.

+ *Review of Prayer:* I record in my journal the insights and understandings that have come to me regarding my journey toward greater spiritual freedom, with special awareness for the feelings that were present.

Week III, Day 6: How Hard It Is!

MARK 10:17–30

He was setting out on a journey when a man ran up, knelt before him and put this question to him, "Good master, what must I do to inherit eternal life?" • Jesus said to him, "Why do you call me good? No one is good but God alone. • You know the commandments: You must not kill; You must not commit adultery; You must not steal; You must not bring false witness; You must not defraud; Honour your father and mother." • And he said to him, "Master, I have kept all these from my earliest days." • Jesus looked steadily at him and loved him, and he said, "There is one thing you lack. Go and sell everything you own and give the money to the poor, and you will have treasure in heaven; then come, follow me." • But his face fell at these words and he went away sad, for he was a man of great wealth.

• Jesus looked round and said to his disciples, "How hard it is for those who have riches to enter the kingdom of God!" • The disciples were astounded by these words, but Jesus insisted, "My children," he said to them, "how hard it is to enter the kingdom of God! • It is easier for a camel to pass through the eye of a needle than for a rich man to enter the kingdom of God." • They were more astonished than ever. "In that case," they said to one another, "who can be saved?" • Jesus gazed at them, "For [humans]," he said, "it is impossible, but not for God: because everything is possible for God."

• Peter took this up. "What about us?" he asked him. "We have left everything and followed you." • Jesus said, "I tell you solemnly, there is no one who has left house, brothers, sisters, father, children or land for my sake and for the sake of the gospel • who will not be repaid a hundred times over, houses brothers, sisters, mothers, children and land—not without

> *persecutions—now in this present time and, in the world to come, eternal life."*

And Jesus, looking upon him, loved him.

What did Jesus see as he looked at the rich man?

He saw a man obviously very wealthy, probably a member of a prominent family (Luke 18:18) who, though seeming to "have everything," projected an image of discontent. In him, Jesus saw a person who was searching for the ultimate meaning of life.

"What must I do . . . ?" the man asked Jesus. The question revealed more about the man's inner attitude than he may have intended. It reflected the direction that had shaped his life to this point in time.

He was very wealthy; he had systematically taken every precaution to assure his security. Not only did he have the status of name and acquired wealth, but he could also claim to have fulfilled all the commandments. His "riches" extended far beyond his material possessions. The defensive pattern of his life had narrowed his vision and, consequently, he had placed all his trust in things and in what he himself could do. "*I* have kept all these. . . ."

In the question he addressed to Jesus, it was as if he were asking, "What is missing? What else is there?"

He was a good man; he had been sincere in keeping the commandments. Undoubtedly, his searching had surfaced from a stirring deep within his heart telling him, "there *is* more."

And Jesus, looking upon him, loved him.

Mark's tender words of Jesus' love reassure all who seek the "more."

With eyes of love, Jesus saw the potential within the man and invited him to enter into a closer relationship. Jesus pointed out to him the one thing lacking, the source of his discontent.

What was that one thing? The man had failed to truly accept himself. He had denied the deepest reality of who he was. He had spent his life proving his worth through what he possessed and what he could do.

The man was out of touch with the ultimate question for every human being. That question was not, "What am I to do?" but, rather, "Who am I in myself, in relationship to God?"

In failing to address this question, the man had effectively closed himself off, not only from his deepest self, but also to the needs of others.

The question he had posed revealed his basic, pervasive lack of trust. Jesus' perceptive response exposed this impoverishment.

"Sell everything that you own and give the money to the poor, and . . . follow me."

Jesus invited the man to become fully himself, by making the "leap beyond himself" (60, p. 403). "But his face fell at these words and he went away sad, for he was a man of great wealth."

These words are among the saddest in Scripture. The man was so filled with himself and his "riches" that he refused to surrender to the greater security. He refused to pass through the dying to himself that would have made possible his experience of peace, of being freed and opened to "everything, to everything without exception; openness to absolute truth, to absolute love, and to the absolute infinity of human life in its immediacy to the very reality which we call God" (60, p. 402).

The man walked away; he was sad.

Jesus, too, must have been saddened, for he commented, "How hard it is for those who have riches to enter the kingdom of God!"

The disciples and we, too, ask, "What about us?"

Jesus assures us that "letting go" is a gift from God. It cannot be accomplished on our own. Only in the recognition of our dependency on God and in the placing of our total trust in God, can we dare to risk the vulnerability demanded by total openness to the harsh, as well as to the beautiful, realities of life.

And Jesus, looking on us, loves us.

Suggested Approach to Prayer: Saying "Yes"

+ *Daily prayer pattern:* (See pages 1 and 2.)
   I quiet myself and relax in the presence of God.
   I declare my dependency on God.

+ *Grace:* I beg for the grace to be free enough to choose from within God's particular call to me, what will *most* clearly radiate and make visible God's goodness in our world.

+ *Method:* Contemplation, as on page 3.

I enter into the story of the rich man who brought his searching question to Jesus. I allow myself to taste of his longings; I image myself in his shoes.

What does it feel like to approach Jesus with his question? Do I approach him hesitantly? fearfully? eagerly? out of curiosity or arrogance?

What is Jesus' expression when he hears my question? Is it one of amazement or tenderness or sadness or is it something else?

I follow the dialogue of the passage carefully, noting the details and the accompanying feelings. I listen as Jesus tells me to sell everything.

I let surface what would be most difficult for me to surrender. I am very aware of any feelings that accompany the thought of letting go.

Contrary to the rich man, I decide to say "yes" to Jesus. I image myself at the moment of the surrender; I face the reality of the cost of such surrendering. I share my feelings about this with Jesus.

I see his response; I pay close attention to his expression and his words.

I beg Jesus to be with me in all this and to direct me further in this decision to follow him.

+ *Closing:* I ask Mary to intercede for me that I would receive the gift of total dependency on God. I ask that I would be so detached from all things that I would put all my talents, possessions, and achievements at the service of Christ. I pray to follow in the pattern of Christ's life—even to the end. Providing it would not be sinful on anyone's part, I pray that if it is God's wish for me, I would have, like Christ, the courage and strength to endure poverty and/or personal humiliation.

I pray the Hail Mary.

In the company of Mary, I approach Jesus and offer the same prayer, that he would obtain these graces for me from my Creator. I pray "Soul of Christ," p. 141.

In the presence of Jesus and Mary, and offered by them, I approach God my Creator. Again I make the same request.

I pray the Our Father.

+ *Review of Prayer:* I write in my journal what has surfaced in my prayer as a call to my closer following of Jesus, attending especially to the feelings that were present.

Week IV, Day 1: Walking in the Spirit

MATTHEW 3:13

Then Jesus appeared: he came from Galilee to the Jordan. . . .

"Home is where one starts from" (24, p. 120).

After having lived at home with Joseph and Mary for nearly thirty years, Jesus "came from Galilee to the Jordan." Within this brief phrase is the untold story of the separation of a child from his parents. It marks the emergence of the young man, Jesus, and his going forth into the world.

It was a time of decision for Jesus, and everything that had come before had prepared him for this moment. Nothing had so readied him as the love and care he had received in the home at Nazareth. In the holding of this love in his heart lay the secret of his openness to life.

The deep fidelity of Mary and Joseph to Yahweh gifted Jesus with the rich spiritual heritage of his ancestral past. All those who had gone before him in faith walked with him now as he made his way to the Jordan.

His faith was the faith of Abraham who had held firm to God's promises in the face of adversity; his longing was that of Moses as he dreamed of the Promised Land; his trust was the trust of his people in exile as, homeless, they had waited and waited.

This deep wellspring of faith provided Jesus with a sense of purpose and direction based on the confidence that, just as God had acted in the past, God would continue to act in the unfolding of Jesus' own life. The promise which had been given to his ancestors gave impetus and significance to his present journey—"a lifetime burning in every moment" (Ibid).

Drawn by the Lord, Jesus walked in the spirit of his people. He walked in the spirit that impelled him forward with the force of love into the realization of his mission and destiny as the Son of God.

Suggested Approach to Prayer: Ball of Life

+ *Daily prayer pattern:* (See pages 1 and 2.)

I quiet myself and relax in the presence of God.
I declare my dependency on God.

+ *Grace:* I ask the grace to appreciate Jesus' deep sense of mission and his human experience of leaving family and home. I ask for the grace to respond in the same Spirit to God's particular call to me.

+ *Method:* Meditation, as on page 3.

My life, like that of Jesus, is one of decision and journey, of leaving the known for the unknown. In the recalling of Jesus' journey from Nazareth to the Jordan, I recall my own.

I gather, as if into a large ball, the memories of my life. Beginning with my childhood, I gather memories of my mother and father, brothers and sisters, of my grandparents. I see again the tender moments of love with them, as well as those moments of pain and disappointment. I gather them all together within the ball, perhaps even moving my hands physically as if to draw them inward.

I move through my life . . . the teen-age years . . . the departure from home . . . and up to the present time. All along the journey I remember the people and the events, the friends of school and college, the happy, successful times and also those times of failure and unhappiness.

As I gather all of these together, I become conscious of the dynamic event my life has been. There are so many people; so much has happened. So many decisions have already occurred, each giving direction and shaping my life.

As I contemplate my ball of life, I become more aware of how similar experiences seem to cluster together in patterns. I take note of the colors and the textures of the clusters. I identify these clusters with a specific word or phrase, for example, times of loss, change, and new growth; important decisions; homelessness; deep relationships, and so forth.

I take my ball of life to Jesus. I show him its many colors and textures. I tell him about it, what it says to me about the pattern of my life, and what it is telling me about the decisions I now am facing. I see Jesus take the ball into his hands. I watch his face as, with love, he looks at each cluster.

I listen to Jesus as he tells me how the clusters interrelate and form a pattern in my life. He tells me how God has been present and active in all the events.

Even those clusters which contain the darkness of pain and/or sin are touched with his mercy and forgiveness. He tells me how the pattern of my life resembles the pattern of his own. In his human experience he, too, was not spared the joys and sufferings of life.

Jesus reassures me, saying that all that has been gathered within my life is held together and made whole in God's love. He tells me that everything in my life has prepared me for the particular call that is mine.

With open arms, I receive my ball of life from Christ.

+ *Closing:* I ask Mary to intercede for me that I would receive the gift of total dependency on God. I ask that I would be so detached from all things that I would put all my talents, possessions, and achievements at the service of Christ. I pray to follow in the pattern of Christ's life—even to the end. Providing it would not be sinful on anyone's part, I pray that if it is God's wish for me, I would have, like Christ, the courage and strength to endure poverty and/or personal humiliation.

I pray the Hail Mary.

In the company of Mary I approach Jesus and offer the same prayer, that he would obtain these graces for me from my Creator. I pray "Soul of Christ," p. 141.

In the presence of Jesus and Mary, and offered by them, I approach God my Creator. Again I make the same request.

I pray the Our Father.

+ *Review of Prayer:* I write in my journal the insights, reflections, and feelings that have surfaced during my prayer.

Week IV, Day 2: This Is My Beloved

MATTHEW 3:13,16–17

Then Jesus appeared: he came from Galilee to the Jordan to be baptised by John.

As soon as Jesus was baptised he came up from the water, and suddenly the heavens opened and he saw the Spirit of God descending like a dove and coming down on him. • And a voice spoke from heaven, "This is my Son, the Beloved; my favour rests on him."

Water and the fire of the Spirit come together in the Baptism of Jesus.

In this climactic experience—past, present, and future converge.

The creative force of the Spirit hovering over the primal chaotic waters (Gen. 1:2) of our being is held in the powerful symbolism of water and fire. The images recall that time when from a pillar of fire, Yahweh protected and led Israel through the Reed Sea into freedom and new birth as God's chosen ones (Exod. 14:15ff).

As Jesus, son of Israel, came up from the water, ". . . he saw the Spirit of God descending. . . ." This was the initiation of Jesus into his particular and extraordinary identity and mission.

Jesus heard the Word of God addressed to him, "This is my Son, the beloved; my favour rests on him."

In those words, the desire and élan of Jesus' life was confirmed.

What a moment that must have been for Jesus. Words that, throughout his whole life, had graced his growing awareness of his God and his people were now addressed to him.

In the words of his father calling him "beloved son," the spirit of Jesus must have been awed with the remembering of Isaac who, as Abraham's "beloved" son, was prepared for sacrifice (Gen. 22:2).

"This is my Son, the Beloved; my favour rests on him." Jesus would have known that the words carried the unspoken connotation of "servant" as well as "son." These words of God were an almost exact rendering of one of the Hebrew

Scripture passages that describe the mysterious servant who would be crushed "with suffering. If he offers his life in atonement . . ." (Isa. 53:10). The beloved one is being called to be servant! "Here is my servant whom I uphold, my chosen one in whom my soul delights" (Isa. 42:1a).

Hearing these words, Jesus undoubtedly was gripped by the full impact of his call to live out the role and mission of the servant."I have endowed him with my spirit that he may bring true justice to the nations" (Isa. 42:1b).

The people had been prepared by John the Baptist. Filled with a new sense of their sinfulness and their need for God, they came from every part of the nation seeking John's baptism of repentance.

Jesus knew his time had come. Already in his heart the words sang out, "I have come to bring fire to the earth, and how I wish it were blazing already! There is a baptism I must still receive, and how great is my distress till it is over" (Luke 12:49–50).

In Jesus, the old creation has given way to the new (2 Cor. 5:17). In Jesus, the on-going birth of every person has been made possible. The way to our personal identity as sons and daughters of God, and to the actualization of the unique servant mission that is the privilege of each, has been opened to us in the life of Jesus.

In the waters of the Jordan, overshadowed by the Spirit, a new and irrevocable thing has happened.

"In the days to come—it is the Lord who speaks—I will pour out my spirit on all [humankind]" (Joel 3:1; Acts 2:17).

Suggested Approach to Prayer: Blessed in Water

+ *Daily prayer pattern:* (See pages 1 and 2.)
   I quiet myself and relax in the presence of God.
   I declare my dependency on God.

+ *Grace:* I ask for the gift of deepening knowledge and intimacy with Jesus so that I may follow him more authentically. I ask for the grace of joy in the words that are spoken to Jesus at the time of his Baptism.

+ *Method:* Centering, as on page 4.
   I go to the Jordan with Jesus. As he steps down into the river, I allow myself, with Jesus, to sink into the water.

I feel the water as I am gradually immersed in it; I am aware of my body as it is slowly covered.

I am particularly aware of the water, that is, whether it is clear and fresh, or muddy and stagnant. I am aware of any feelings that accompany this experience.

I remain with this experience as long as I continue to feel a sense of immersion.

As I come out of the water, I rest on the bank of the river. I speak with Christ of his experience and my own.

In a spirit of renewing my Baptism, I pray the following blessing:

God, you give us grace through sacramental signs
    which tell us of the wonder of your unseen power.
In baptism we use your gift of water,
    which you have made a rich symbol
    of the grace you give us in this sacrament.
At the very dawn of creation
    your Spirit breathed on the waters,
    making them the wellspring of all holiness.
In the great flood waters
    you gave us a sign of the waters of Baptism,
    making an end of sin and a new beginning of goodness.
Through the waters of the Reed Sea
    you led Israel out of slavery,
    to be an image of God's holy people,
    set free from sin by Baptism.
In the waters of the Jordan
    your Son was baptized by John
    and anointed with the Spirit.
Your Son willed that water and blood
    should flow from his side
    as he hung upon the cross.
After his resurrection he told his disciples:
    "Go out and teach all nations,

baptizing them in the name of the Father
and of the Son and of the Holy Spirit."
God, our Creator, look now upon your Church and upon me
and unseal the fountain of Baptism.
By the power of the Spirit
give to this water
the grace of your Son.
You created me in your own likeness;
cleanse me from sin in a new birth of innocence
by water and the Spirit.
I ask you, Lord God, with your Son
to send the Holy Spirit upon me.
Springs of water, bless the Lord.
Give the Lord glory and praise forever.

—Easter Vigil: Blessing of Water
(54, pp. 201–202, modified)

+ *Closing:* I ask Mary to intercede for me that I would receive the gift of total dependency on God. I ask that I would be so detached from all things that I would put all my talents, possessions, and achievements at the service of Christ. I pray to follow in the pattern of Christ's life—even to the end. Providing it would not be sinful on anyone's part, I pray that if it is God's wish for me, I would have, like Christ, the courage and strength to endure poverty and/or personal humiliation.

I pray the Hail Mary.

In the company of Mary I approach Jesus and offer the same prayer, that he would obtain these graces for me from my Creator. I pray "Soul of Christ," p. 141.

In the presence of Jesus and Mary, and offered by them, I approach God my Creator. Again I make the same request.

I pray the Our Father.

+ *Review of Prayer:* I write in my journal what has surfaced in my prayer as a call to my closer following of Jesus, attending especially to the feelings that were present.

Week IV, Day 3: True Justice

ISAIAH 42:1–9

Here is my servant whom I uphold,
my chosen one in whom my soul delights.
I have endowed him with my spirit
that he may bring true justice to the nations.

He does not cry out or shout aloud,
or make his voice heard in the streets.
He does not break the crushed reed,
nor quench the wavering flame.

Faithfully he brings true justice;
he will neither waver, nor be crushed
until true justice is established on earth,
for the islands are awaiting his law.

Thus says God, Yahweh,
he who created the heavens and spread them out,
who gave shape to the earth and what comes from it,
who gave breath to its people
and life to the creatures that move in it:

I Yahweh, have called you to serve the cause of right;
I have taken you by the hand and formed you;
I have appointed you as covenant of the people and light
    of the nations,

to open the eyes of the blind,
to free captives from prison,
and those who live in darkness from the dungeon.

My name is Yahweh,
I will not yield my glory to another,
nor my honour to idols.

See how former predictions have come true.

Fresh things I now foretell;
before they appear I tell you of them.

"Hope is absolutely essential to the sanity and wholenes of life" (35, p. 3).

Timeless in their message, the words of Isaiah issue a call for the renewal of a spirit of hope. It is inconceivable that any people or age could have had a greater need for these prophetic words than our own.

Originally, this prophecy of Isaiah was addressed to the Israelites when they were in Babylon, exiled from their homeland. After suffering seventy years of homelessness and yearning, their first real hope appeared in the leadership of Cyrus, the new emperor of Persia (Isa. 41:1–7). He was Yahweh's "shepherd" and was destined to accomplish God's purpose in restoring to the Jewish people their experience of being God's chosen ones (Isa. 44:28).

By permitting the people to return home to Judea and encouraging them to rebuild the Temple in Jerusalem, Cyrus opened new possibilities for the people (2 Chron. 36:22–23). They would rediscover their identity and mission as "light to the nations."

In this new situation, the prophet called his people to a courageous life of enduring selflessness based on total trust in Yahweh. It was a *call* to live in the Spirit of God; it was a call to be servant.

This summons to servanthood was not unfamiliar to the Israelites. It echoed the very essence of their faith. Only in service to God and to others would authentic freedom be actualized.

Within the drama of human history, the prophet Isaiah traced the action of God, as the people of Israel were delivered into freedom. From whatever bondage or blindness was present, the liberation was always collective *and* individual.

Just as Yahweh had drawn the people out of slavery in Egypt through the desert into the promised land, now, in a new Exodus, God was drawing the people out of exile and again through the wilderness (Isa. 43).

In this return from exile, the prophet recalled God's creative energy drawing the universe into being. The Spirit that hovered over the chaos (Gen. 1:2–5), giving birth to the world, was now birthing the emergence of a new reality based on an unlimited trust in God.

"Your salvation lay in conversion and tranquility, your strength, in complete trust . . ." (Isa. 30:15).

Isaiah, the prophet, has done for us, as for the people of Israel, a marvelous deed. In the remembrance and retelling of their story, he has linked the present with the past and thereby impelled Israel forward in hope. An awareness of how God has been faithful in the past and how God is active and involved in the present provides us with the momentum essential for the leap of consciousness which is the core of all hopefulness and new birth.

"See how former predictions have come true. Fresh things I now foretell. . . ."

Isaiah personified hope in the image of the servant. In the four servant songs, the servant is represented, at once, as an autonomous individual and as the community of Israel. Isaiah 42:1–9 is the first of the four songs in which the themes of hope and service are integrated and offered as the way to true justice. This justice is the gift realized by those who live their lives in creative fidelity to the living Word of God. To be just is to be righteous, that is, to be right with God.

In concrete terminology, Isaiah spells out for us the style and tenor of the servant. Endowed with the Spirit, the way of the servant is in direct contrast to that which characterizes military force or imperial power. Where there is violence, he is gentle; where there is blindness, he restores sight; where there is imprisonment, he brings liberation. The servant's life is one of defenselessness. In his total reliance on God, he boldly encounters despair and suffering and thereby witnesses to and inspires hope.

This hope is integrally linked with trust, which necessitates a patient waiting. Trust and hope are not attained through one's own efforts. To grasp, to possess, to seize, is contrary to the way of the servant. Trust and hope are given as pure and ever-new gifts from God and realized only by those who know how to wait.

> He gives power to the faint
> and to those who have no might he increases strength. . . .
> . . . .
> They who wait for the Lord shall renew their strength.
> They shall mount up with wings like eagles.
> They shall run and not be weary,
> they shall walk and not faint. (Isa. 40:29–31 RSV)

Suggested Approach to Prayer: Praying the Song of the Servant

+ *Daily prayer pattern:* (See pages 1 and 2.)
I quiet myself and relax in the presence of God.
I declare my dependency on God.

+ *Grace:* I ask for the gift of a deepening awareness of the spirit and dream that shaped the identity of Jesus so that knowing him more deeply I may follow him more closely.

+ *Method:* Contemplation, as on page 3.
I am aware that Jesus loved, read, and reflected on the Hebrew Scriptures.
I image Jesus in his room, or perhaps on a hillside near a lake, as he reverently reads and reflects on this passage from Isaiah.
I draw closer to Jesus, and, looking up, he invites me to sit near him. I listen quietly as he reads Isaiah 42:1–9. He pauses to repeat some lines, and comments on what the words mean to him and for me, offering prayer to God.
I am aware of the feelings that stir within my heart and the dreams that are awakened within my spirit.

+ *Closing:* I ask Mary to intercede for me that I would receive the gift of total dependency on God. I ask that I would be so detached from all things that I would put all my talents, possessions, and achievements at the service of Christ. I pray to follow in the pattern of Christ's life—even to the end. Providing it would not be sinful on anyone's part, I pray that if it is God's wish for me, I would have, like Christ, the courage and strength to endure poverty and/or personal humiliation.
I pray the Hail Mary.
In the company of Mary I approach Jesus and offer the same prayer, that he would obtain these graces for me from my Creator. I pray "Soul of Christ," p. 141.
In the presence of Jesus and Mary, and offered by them, I approach God my Creator. Again I make the same request.
I pray the Our Father.

+ *Review of Prayer:* I write in my journal the feelings that have surfaced and the thoughts that particularly touched me.

Week IV, Day 4: Evil Is Real

MATTHEW 4:1–11

Then Jesus was led by the Spirit out into the wilderness to be tempted by the devil. • He fasted for forty days and forty nights, after which he was very hungry, • and the tempter came and said to him, "If you are the Son of God, tell these stones to turn into loaves." • But he replied, "Scripture says:

> Man does not live on bread alone
> but on every word that comes from the mouth of God."

The devil then took him to the holy city and made him stand on the parapet of the Temple. • "If you are the Son of God," he said, "throw yourself down; for scripture says:

> He will put you in his angels' charge,
> and they will support you on their hands
> in case you hurt your foot against a stone."

Jesus said to him, "Scripture also says:

> You must not put the Lord your God to the test."

Next, taking him to a very high mountain, the devil showed him all the kingdoms of the world and their splendour. • "I will give you all these," he said, "if you fall at my feet and worship me." • Then Jesus replied, "Be off, Satan! For scripture says:

> You must worship the Lord your God,
> and serve him alone."

Then the devil left him, and angels appeared and looked after him.

Evil is real! Lack of trust is its expression. It speaks with a voice of doubt—doubt of God and doubt of God's presence within oneself.

Jesus encountered this voice in the desert. It was not by chance that this encounter occurred immediately following his Baptism.

"Led by the Spirit," like Moses and Elijah before him, Jesus entered the wilderness to contemplate God's plan for him as the "beloved Son."

What an opportune time for the devil to attack!

Having just been baptized, having received a new level of awareness of who he was and what he was to do, Jesus, in his humanness, was particularly vulnerable to the seductiveness of doubt. One can imagine the devil's panic before the possibility of such a power for goodness about to be released into the world. Satan's desperation became apparent in the absurd—though real—enticements he placed before Jesus.

The temptations of Satan targeted the very center of the identity of Jesus. Would Jesus accept his humanity or would he surrender himself and his love for the human community in exchange for some special powers and protection? In order to assure the success of his mission, would Jesus be obedient enough to trust God's unfolding plan or would he, as Son of God, in an inflated manner, take the power into his own hands?

"If you are the son of God, tell these stones to turn into loaves."

The test began with the most elemental of all needs. Jesus was hungry after having fasted for "forty days and forty nights." In effect, the devil said, "You don't have to be hungry anymore."

This first temptation touches deeply into the human experience of hunger. Jesus' physical hunger is symbolic of the yearnings, the "hunger" of every human heart.

Had Jesus succumbed to being a "quick fix" messiah, he would have negated the mysterious workings of God that are met and mediated within the embracing of one's interior hungering.

One "does not live on bread alone but on every word that comes from the mouth of God."

Zeroing in on Jesus' declaration of his dependency on God, Satan took him to the parapet of the temple. There on the edge, he said,

If you are the Son of God, . . . throw yourself down."

The devious purpose of Satan in the second temptation was to have Jesus destroy himself. Once again, the temptation is for Jesus to deny his humanness and to "cling" to his divinity (Phil. 2:6).

As he stood on that precarious ledge of the precipice, urged to call upon the angels for protection, Jesus' test was not so unlike our own temptations to force God's hand.

Jesus, too, must stand alone in total trust. He, too, must endure the loneliness and seeming futility that is integral to the human journey toward authenticity of self in God. To deny this darkness would be to forfeit the discovery of self and, indeed, to destroy oneself.

Jesus did not deny the darkness; he did not plunge himself into an attention-getting display that would have been not only a false attempt to prove his holiness and power, but also an abuse of God's promise of protection (Ps. 91:11–12).

"You must not put the Lord your God to the test."

The efforts of Satan escalated and reached their climax at the point when Jesus was tempted with having authority over the whole world.

"I will give you all these . . . if you fall at my feet and worship me."

Direct and blatant, this temptation to power brought Jesus face to face with the cosmic struggle that each person encounters. The question is simple: Who do you choose—God or Satan?

The human response, however, is not so simple and is often cloaked in the subtleties of compromise. Our inner dialogue may sound like this: In order to achieve this good, I need to "sacrifice" this truth; or, in order to maintain peace, I must be silent. Whenever one allows one's being to be dictated to or controlled by another, a progressive sellout of oneself occurs. The result is always a loss of freedom.

That "other" can be a person, project, goal, idea, even a molten calf, as it was for the Israelites (Exod. 32). Whatever or whomever absorbs and distorts one's authentic freedom becomes an idol and sets into motion a tragic travesty of love.

Jesus would have none of this. With clarity of vision, he decisively dismissed the devil. "Be off, Satan!"

In doing so, Jesus claimed his identity of self as beloved Son.

Having met and unmasked the evil forces that challenged his Sonship, Jesus was ready to begin his ministry of love.

Suggested Approach to Prayer: Into the Wilderness

+ *Daily prayer pattern:* (See pages 1 and 2.)

93

I quiet myself and relax in the presence of God.
I declare my dependency on God.

+ *Grace:* I ask for the gift of growing inner knowledge and intimacy with Jesus so that I may follow him more closely. I ask for a deep appreciation of his humanity and for a growing trust and faith as a sharing in Jesus' total dependence on the Lord God.

+ *Method:* Contemplation, as on page 3.

I go with Jesus into the wilderness. I image in great detail the physical surroundings in which I find myself. What is it that comprises *my* wilderness? Do I find myself in a desert, or is the image of my wilderness a dark forest, or a frozen tundra or an empty house or . . . ?

I take note of my feelings as I stand in the midst of this wilderness to which I have been led. I become aware of what I am experiencing as most oppressive, most fearful and threatening and confusing.

I become aware of the presence of evil. I look closely at that presence. I allow an image of it to take shape; perhaps it is a dark shadow, or a threatening animal, or a "devil" person, or a disembodied voice. I watch this evil presence, becoming aware of how it moves, how it looks, how it speaks.

I hear this evil presence address me with the three temptations addressed to Jesus.

It speaks to my "hunger": "You don't have to be hungry any more."

It speaks to my need for the support and approval of others: "There are 'ways' to get around things to achieve what you want—to get attention, praise, and prove youself."

It speaks to my need to be who I am: "Your power and control is the measure of your worth."

As I consider each of these temptations, I become aware that Jesus is with me. I speak to him about my temptations and ask him to share with me his strength so that I will not succumb to the evil.

I thank Jesus for having entered so deeply into the human and humble experience of being tempted.

+ *Closing:* I ask Mary to intercede for me that I would receive the gift of total dependency on God. I ask that I would be so detached from all things that I would put all my talents, possessions, and achievements at the service of Christ. I pray to follow in the pattern of Christ's life—even to the end. Providing it would not be sinful on anyone's part, I pray that if it is God's wish for me, I would have, like Christ, the courage and strength to endure poverty and/or personal humiliation.

I pray the Hail Mary.

In the company of Mary, I approach Jesus and offer the same prayer, that he would obtain these graces for me from my Creator. I pray "Soul of Christ," p. 141.

In the presence of Jesus and Mary, and offered by them, I approach God my Creator. Again I make the same request.

I pray the Our Father.

+ *Review of Prayer:* I record in my journal the insights and feelings that have surfaced during this period of prayer.

Week IV, Day 5: An Inaugural Statement

LUKE 4:16–30

He came to Nazara, where he had been brought up, and went into the synagogue on the sabbath day as he usually did. He stood up to read, • and they handed him the scroll of the prophet Isaiah. Unrolling the scroll he found the place where it is written:

> The spirit of the Lord has been given to me,
> for he has anointed me.
> He has sent me to bring the good news to the poor,
> to proclaim liberty to captives
> and to the blind new sight,
> to set the downtrodden free,
> to proclaim the Lord's year of favour.

He then rolled up the scroll, gave it back to the assistant and sat down. And all eyes in the synagogue were fixed on him. • Then he began to speak to them, "This text is being fulfilled today even as you listen." • And he won the approval of all, and they were astonished by the gracious words that came from his lips.

They said, "This is Joseph's son, surely?" • But he replied, "No doubt you will quote me the saying, 'Physician, heal yourself' and tell me, 'We have heard all that happened in Capernaum, do the same here in your own countryside.'" And he went on, "I tell you solemnly, no prophet is ever accepted in his own country.

"There were many widows in Israel, I can assure you, in Elijah's day, when heaven remained shut for three years and six months and a great famine raged throughout the land, • but Elijah was not sent to any one of these: he was sent to a widow at Zarephath, a Sidonian town. And in the prophet Elisha's time there were many lepers in Israel, but none of these was cured, except the Syrian, Naaman."

*When they heard this everyone in the synagogue was
enraged. • They sprang to their feet and hustled him out of the
town; and they took him up to the brow of the hill their town
was built on, intending to throw him down the cliff, • but he
slipped through the crowd and walked away.*

What is impressive about this passage is the courage of Jesus!

His response to and trust in the presence of the Spirit within himself enabled
Jesus to begin his ministry with remarkable boldness.

Among his own people, in the midst of family and friends, he was invited, as
guest of honor, to participate in the Sabbath synagogue service. Jesus read from
Isaiah. We will never know if the selection was by deliberate choice or by chance.

What we *do* know is that what was originally intended as a recitation com-
memorating the past was experienced by Jesus in his actual reading of it as the
reality present within himself. What had identified Isaiah now identified Jesus.

"This text is being fulfilled today even as you listen."

The word had broken free and spanned time; Jesus and the people who
listened were carried beyond themselves! Such a leap transpires only under the
persuasion of the Spirit!

The immediate response of the people was one of delight and pride as they
enthusiastically claimed Jesus as "Joseph's son," one of their own.

Jesus, however, did not allow himself the indulgence of their admiration, nor
would he succumb to any self-serving demands they might attempt to impose.

Firmly and decisively, he clarified his understanding of what his own
ministry would entail. Just as Elijah and Elisha served beyond the borders of
Israel, so, too, would his ministry reach beyond *his* people and *this* place. His
ministry, like God's love, would be totally unconditional and extend to all.

On hearing this, the mood of the people shifted dramatically! They became
"enraged" when they realized that not only had Jesus identified himself with the
passage from Isaiah, but that they were not to be the exclusive focus of his
ministry. Jesus' ministry was to be shared even with the Gentiles who traditionally
had been the object of Jewish ridicule and hostility.

In making his inaugural statement, Jesus had courageously contradicted centuries of blatant nationalism. He, in effect, had reclaimed the universality of Isaiah's prophetic challenge:

I will make you the light of the nations
so that my salvation may reach to the ends of the earth. (Isa. 49:6b)

The contradiction incited the people to violence. They were prepared even to kill him.

"But he slipped through the crowd and walked away." Their limited vision could not hold him bound.

This episode is a recapitulation of the entire ministry of Jesus. As in a microcosm, we see the pattern of acceptance and rejection that characterized his life.

In each of our lives and in the measure proportionate to our personal surrender to the Spirit of our Baptism, this pattern is "re-presented." As Isaiah's words became the words of Jesus, the words and experience of Jesus become our own.

Suggested Approach to Prayer: Courage of Jesus

+ *Daily prayer pattern:* (See pages 1 and 2.)
  I quiet myself and relax in the presence of God.
  I declare my dependency on God.

+ *Grace:* I ask for the grace of a deepening knowledge and intimacy with Jesus, especially for a share in his courage and trust and an appreciation for his humanity.

+ *Method:* Contemplation, as on page 3.
  I accompany Jesus into the synagogue of Nazareth.
  I image in great detail the synagogue and envison the people present. I watch the faces of the assembled people as Jesus reads the words of Isaiah. I, too, watch his face as he reads, and I listen.
  I enter deeply into the Spirit of Jesus in the ensuing dialogue. I become particularly aware of the courage of Jesus as he defines his ministry. I see his response to the hostility of his townspeople.

In the presence of Jesus, I reflect on my own courage or lack of courage
- to claim my personal identity,
- to trust in the Spirit present within me,
- to surrender in obedience to God's will as revealed in my situation and the circumstances of life,
- to face rejection, even, possibly, from those I most love.

+ *Closing:* I ask Mary to intercede for me that I would receive the gift of total dependency on God. I ask that I would be so detached from all things that I would put all my talents, possessions, and achievements at the service of Christ. I pray to follow in the pattern of Christ's life—even to the end. Providing it would not be sinful on anyone's part, I pray that if it is God's wish for me, I would have, like Christ, the courage and strength to endure poverty and/or personal humiliation.

I pray the Hail Mary.

In the company of Mary, I approach Jesus and offer the same prayer, that he would obtain these graces for me from my Creator. I pray "Soul of Christ," p. 141.

In the presence of Jesus and Mary, and offered by them, I approach God my Creator. Again I make the same request.

I pray the Our Father.

+ *Review of Prayer:* I write in my journal the reflections and feelings that have surfaced during this period of prayer.

Week IV, Day 6: Repetition

Suggested Approach to Prayer

+ *Daily prayer pattern:* (See pages 1 and 2.)
I quiet myself and relax in the presence of God.
I declare my dependency on God.

+ *Grace:* I ask to know Jesus more intimately, to love him more deeply, and to follow him more closely.

+ *Method:* Repetition, as on page 6.
In preparation, I review my previous prayer periods by reading my journal since the last repetition day. I select for my repetition the period of prayer in which I was most deeply moved or the one in which I experienced a lack of emotional response. I use the method with which I approached the passage initially. I open myself to hear again God's word to me in that particular passage.

+ *Review of Prayer:* I write in my journal any feelings, experiences, or insights that have surfaced in this "second listening."

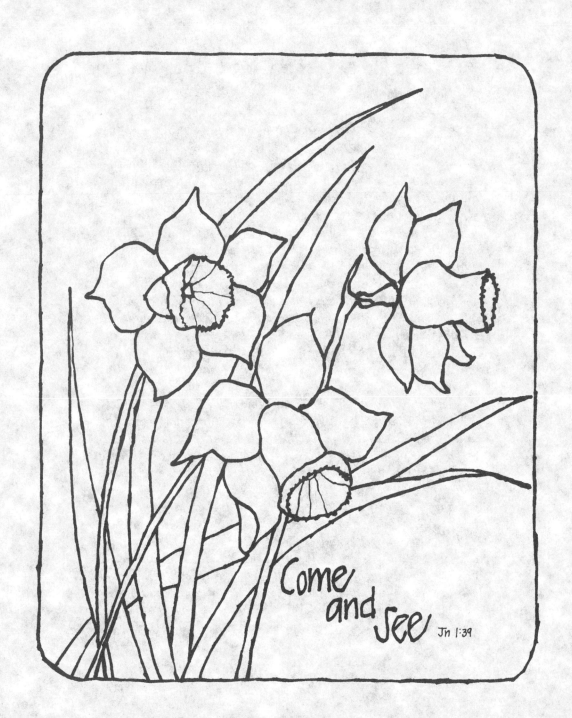

Come and see

Jn 1:39

Week V, Day 1: Come and See

JOHN 1:35–51

On the following day as John stood there again with two of his disciples, Jesus passed, and John stared hard at him and said, "Look, there is the lamb of God." • Hearing this, the two disciples followed Jesus. • Jesus turned round, saw them following and said, "What do you want?" They answered, "Rabbi,"—which means Teacher—"where do you live?" • "Come and see," he replied; so they went and saw where he lived, and stayed with him the rest of that day. It was about the tenth hour.

One of these two who became followers of Jesus after hearing what John had said was Andrew, the brother of Simon Peter. • Early next morning, Andrew met his brother and said to him, "We have found the Messiah"—which means the Christ—• and he took Simon to Jesus. Jesus looked hard at him and said, "You are Simon, son of John; you are to be called Cephas"—meaning Rock.

The next day, after Jesus had decided to leave for Galilee, he met Philip and said, "Follow me." • Philip came from the same town, Bethsaida, as Andrew and Peter. • Philip found Nathanael and said to him, "We have found the one Moses wrote about in the Law, the one about whom the prophets wrote: he is Jesus, son of Joseph, from Nazareth." • "From Nazareth?" said Nathanael. "Can anything good come from that place?" "Come and see," replied Philip. • When Jesus saw Nathanael coming he said of him, "There is an Israelite who deserves the name, incapable of deceit." • "How do you know me?" said Nathanael. "Before Philip came to call you," said Jesus, "I saw you under the fig tree." • Nathanael answered, "Rabbi, you are the Son of God, you are the King of Israel." • Jesus replied, "You believe that just because I said: I saw you under the fig tree. You will see greater things than that." • And then he added, "I tell you most solemnly, you will see heaven laid open and, above the Son of Man, the angels of God ascending and descending."

Latent—and sometimes locked—within each human heart is a dream waiting to be born.

Jesus is the key which frees this unawakened desire to the reality of human expression. He is the one who asks, "What do you want?"

This vital, initiating question stirs into awareness the basic longing inherent in every human being.

The historical reality that God did, in fact, become human in Jesus has intrinsically affected and altered all of creation. From the first moment of coming into being, each person is gifted with a share in the life of Jesus.

Whatever degree of awareness may ultimately be attained, this initial gift of grace continues to exert upon each individual a creative energy that provides an openness to receive the deeper reality of his or her particular destiny in Christ. It is what prompts one to seek and to ask, "Where do you live?"

The response of Jesus to this question of John and Andrew was, "Come and see."

They went, and saw, and stayed!

The decision to actively follow and stay with Jesus was the beginning of their discipleship.

In the apocryphal *Acts of John*, the early Church remembered Jesus saying,

A Lamp am I to you that perceive me. Amen.
A mirror am I to you that know me. Amen. (74, p. 168)

By looking at Jesus and listening to his words, the two disciples gradually came to an understanding of Jesus. As in a mirror, they looked at him and were enabled to envision their own deepest reality, a reality which brought them face to face with the source of their being.

"To have seen me is to have seen the Father" (John 14:9).

With the realization of who Jesus was, the hopes of the Hebrew Scriptures came to life for the disciples. In Jesus they saw the One about whom Moses wrote, the King of Israel. The dreams of Israel and their own dreams had taken on new possibilities for fulfillment; what they had long awaited now seemed actually in sight. The preparation of John the Baptist had led them to this acknowledgment. Jesus was the Lamb of God, the Suffering Servant, the Messiah!

With new and irrepressible zeal, they enthusiastically spread the news of Jesus and unleashed a powerful energy that created and gave form to the network of believers who comprised the early Church community.

The call of Jesus reached from John and Andrew to Peter, and through the centuries it has reached out to each of us.

Just as Peter experienced a radical transformation, symbolized by his change of name, we, too, are given the potential of new life. As Nathanael thrilled to Jesus' special inner knowledge of him, we, too, can rejoice in the assurance that our most secret dreams are known by Christ.

Within each of us is Jesus' dream of our discipleship. *His* dream for us is more than we can possibly imagine.

Make ready for the Christ whose smile like lightning sets free the song of everlasting glory that now sleeps in your paper flesh like dynamite. (Thomas Merton)

Suggested Approach to Prayer: The Invitation

+ *Daily prayer pattern:* (See pages 1 and 2.)
  I quiet myself and relax in the presence of God.
  I declare my dependency on God.

+ *Grace:* I ask for the gift of knowing Jesus more fully, to love him more intimately, so as to follow him more closely.

+ *Method:* Contemplation, as on page 3.
  I prayerfully reread the passage.
  I see myself as one of the disciples; I image myself in front of Jesus. I hear him say to me, "What is it you want?"
  Like the other disciples, I ask him, "Where do you live?"
  I go where Jesus leads me. I spend time with him. I listen attentively to his words to me. I watch his movements and manner of response.

I share with him what I see and hear as I look at and listen to him.

I ask him what it is I need to do to be more like him, and I listen to his response.

+ *Closing:* I ask Mary to intercede for me that I would receive the gift of total dependency on God. I ask that I would be so detached from all things that I would put all my talents, possessions, and achievements at the service of Christ. I pray to follow in the pattern of Christ's life—even to the end. Providing it would not be sinful on anyone's part, I pray that if it is God's wish for me, I would have, like Christ, the courage and strength to endure poverty and/or personal humiliation.

I pray the Hail Mary.

In the company of Mary I approach Jesus and offer the same prayer, that he would obtain these graces for me from my Creator. I pray "Soul of Christ," p. 141.

In the presence of Jesus and Mary, and offered by them, I approach God my Creator. Again I make the same request.

I pray the Our Father.

+ *Review of Prayer:* I record in my journal images, insights, and feelings that have arisen within me during this time of prayer.

Week V, Day 2: Cana Is Now

JOHN 2:1–11

Three days later there was a wedding at Cana in Galilee. The mother of Jesus was there, and Jesus and his disciples had also been invited. When they ran out of wine, since the wine provided for the wedding was all finished, the mother of Jesus said to him, "They have no wine." • Jesus said, "Woman, why turn to me? My hour has not come yet." • His mother said to the servants, "Do whatever he tells you." • There were six stone water jars standing there, meant for the ablutions that are customary among the Jews: each could hold twenty or thirty gallons. • Jesus said to the servants, "Fill the jars with water," and they filled them to the brim. • "Draw some out now," he told them "and take it to the steward." • They did this; the steward tasted the water, and it had turned into wine. Having no idea where it came from—only the servants who had drawn the water knew—the steward called the bridegroom • and said, "People generally serve the best wine first, and keep the cheaper sort till the guests have had plenty to drink; but you have kept the best wine till now."

This was the first of the signs given by Jesus; it was given at Cana in Galilee. He let his glory be seen, and his disciples believed in him.

When the waters saw, you O God,
When the waters saw you, they were afraid, the deep trembled.

You are the God who works wonders,
Who has manifested your might. (Ps. 77:14,16, RSV)

Moved by the power of God, the waters of the Reed Sea became, for the people of the Hebrew Scriptures, a path to liberation. At the onset of the new age, the waters of Cana, touched by the power of Christ's word, were transformed into the choicest wine and became for all time a sign of the joy and fulfillment of the promise.

The miracle of water changed into wine was meant to lead the disciples to an inner enlightenment and appreciation of Jesus and the power given to him by God. The object of the miracle was not to fixate our attention on the wondrous external event of water into wine but, rather, to see in the miracle the deeper reality that is not readily visible. In the perception and consequent belief in this deeper reality lies our own meaning and blessedness.

In other words, "what is demanded is not faith in miracles, but faith in Jesus and in him whom Jesus has revealed" (43, p. 237).

The remarkable transformation of water and wine was the first of several signs John used to illustrate the power and presence of Christ. In each of the miracles that followed, Jesus was shown as the fulfillment of the Hebrew Scripture promises.

In the coming of Christ, "the world of the past has gone" (Rev. 21:4b). What had previously given meaning—Jewish feasts and ritual practices—was not superceded by Christ himself.

Jesus declared himself to be the temple (John 2:19); Jesus is the bread of life (John 6:35); Jesus is the light of the world (John 8:12). He alone has become the way to God.

And his disciples believed in him.

In witnessing the miracle of Cana, the disciples' faith and belief in Jesus was given new impetus. The miraculous event, occurring as it did, at the celebration of a wedding, readied the hearts of the disciples to be opened to Jesus. The marriage feast already held great symbolism for the disciples, as it did for all the Israelites, as an image of the future kingdom when all would be united in peace with God. Within this joyful context the disciples were able to recognize and to accept Jesus as the Messiah, the one who would bring about this union, the Kingdom.

Among those who attended the wedding was Mary, the mother of Jesus, who exemplified this belief in Jesus. She had "pondered" it in her heart for years. When Mary realized there was a shortage of wine, her dynamic faith prompted her to boldly make an appeal to the resourcefulness of Jesus. She urged her son to begin his mission at once.

Her daring initiative set into motion, not only the change of water to wine, but the transformation of her own relationship with Jesus. Jesus called his mother "woman," a term of respect that was indicative of her role in his ministry. At the foot of the cross, she would receive the Church in the person of John (John 19:25–27) and tradition would later claim her as "mother of the church." She was the new Eve (1, *The Church*, Par. 53, 86).

We, like Mary and the disciples, live in the new age and are participants in the new creation. Through the power of Christ's words, the ordinariness of our daily lives is transformed into the wine of his presence.

Cana is now!

Suggested Approach to Prayer: At the Wedding

+ *Daily prayer pattern:* (See pages 1 and 2.)
I quiet myself and relax in the presence of God.
I declare my dependency on God.

+ *Grace:* I ask to know Jesus more fully, to love him more intimately, to follow him more closely.

+ *Method:* Contemplation, as on page 3.
I reread prayerfully the passage, aware of the story and the images. I see myself as one of the servants at the wedding.

I see the bridal couple, beautiful in their joy in each other.

I image the festive surroundings—guests, food, music. I experience the atmosphere of celebration that envelops the occasion—joy, excitement, laughter.

I share in the anxiety regarding the impending shortage of wine. I see Mary approach Jesus, and I listen to their exchange.

I hear Mary issue orders to us, the servants. I assist in filling the jars with water. I am the one chosen to bring a sample to the wine steward.

I observe as he exclaims, then proclaims it as the "choicest wine."

I am aware of my own feelings as I witness this manifestation of Jesus' power.

I reflect on what this power of Jesus holds for me in the circumstances of my life.

+ *Closing:* I ask Mary to intercede for me that I would receive the gift of total dependency on God. I ask that I would be so detached from all things that I would put all my talents, possessions, and achievements at the service of Christ. I pray to follow in the pattern of Christ's life—even to the end. Providing it would not be sinful on anyone's part, I pray that if it is God's wish for me, I would have, like Christ, the courage and strength to endure poverty and/or personal humiliation.

I pray the Hail Mary.

In the company of Mary, I approach Jesus and offer the same prayer, that he would obtain these graces for me from my Creator. I pray "Soul of Christ," p. 141.

In the presence of Jesus and Mary, and offered by them, I approach God my Creator. Again I make the same request.

I pray the Our Father.

+ *Review of Prayer:* In my journal I record the feelings that have arisen within me during my prayer, the words that touched me.

Week V, Day 3: The Living Water

JOHN 4:5–30,39–42

On the way he came to the Samaritan town called Sychar, near the land that Jacob gave to his son Joseph. • *Joseph's well is there and Jesus, tired by the journey, sat straight down by the well. It was about the sixth hour.* • *When a Samaritan woman came to draw water, Jesus said to her, "Give me a drink." His disciples had gone into the town to buy food.* • *The Samaritan woman said to him, "What? You are a Jew and you ask me, a Samaritan, for a drink?"—Jews, in fact, do not associate with Samaritans.* • *Jesus replied:*

> *"If you only knew what God is offering*
> *and who it is that is saying to you:*
> *'Give me a drink,'*
> *you would have been the one to ask,*
> *and he would have given you living water."*

"You have no bucket, sir," she answered "and the well is deep: how could you get this living water? • *Are you a greater man than our father Jacob who gave us this well and drank from it himself with his sons and his cattle?"* • *Jesus replied:*

> *"Whoever drinks this water*
> *will get thirsty again;*
> *but anyone who drinks the water that I shall give*
> *will never be thirsty again;*
> *the water that I shall give*
> *will turn into a spring inside him, welling up to eternal life."*

"Sir," said the woman "give me some of that water, so that I may never get thirsty and never have to come here again to draw water." • *"Go and call your husband," said Jesus to her "and come back here."* • *The woman answered, "I have no*

110

husband." He said to her, "You are right to say, 'I have no husband;' • for although you have had five, the one you have now is not your husband. You spoke the truth there." • "I see you are a prophet, sir" said the woman. • "Our fathers worshipped on this mountain, while you say that Jerusalem is the place where one ought to worship." • Jesus said:

"Believe me, woman, the hour is coming
when you will worship the Father
neither on this mountain nor in Jerusalem.
You worship what you do not know;
we worship what we do know;
for salvation comes from the Jews.
But the hour will come—in fact is is here already—
when true worshippers will worship the Father in spirit
    and truth:
that is the kind of worshipper
the Father wants.
God is spirit,
and those who worship
must worship in spirit and truth."

The woman said to him, "I know that Messiah—that is, Christ—is coming; and when he comes he will tell us everything." • "I who am speaking to you," said Jesus, "I am he."

At this point his disciples returned, and were surprised to find him speaking to a woman, though none of them asked, "What do you want from her?" or, "Why are you talking to her?" • The woman put down her water jar and hurried back to the town to tell the people, " • Come and see a man who has told me everything I ever did; I wonder if he is the Christ?" • This brought people out of the town and they started walking towards him. . . .

Many Samaritans of that town had believed in him on the strength of the woman's testimony when she said, "He told me

111

all I have ever done," • so, when the Samaritans came up to him, they begged him to stay with them. He stayed for two days, and • when he spoke to them many more came to believe; • and they said to the woman, "Now we no longer believe because of what you told us; we have heard him ourselves and we know that he really is the saviour of the world."

"Come and see a man that told me everything I ever did; I wonder if he is the Christ?"

The exuberance of the woman after her encounter with Jesus at the well is present in her eagerness to share with others her new vision of life.

Come and see . . . is he the Christ?

Having gone to the well to replenish her supply of water, she was faced with her own inner thirst. Ironically this realization was precipitated by the thirst of Jesus.

"Give me a drink." This simple human request from one in need, and the simple human response of one who could serve that need introduced the woman to the person who would tell her "everything."

She was not at all prepared for her meeting with Christ. As a woman, she expected to be ignored, yet Jesus spoke words that pierced the very depths of her soul. As a Samaritan she anticipated, from any Jew, only hostility; from Jesus she received understanding and respect.

The woman offered Jesus water from the well; he offered her a spring of living water.

This living water is the Spirit of God dwelling within each one of us. The Spirit waits only to be freed, freed to flow into, to cleanse, and to replenish every facet of our lives. With God our Creator as its source, this living water, the Spirit, renews with creative blessing all our thoughts, actions, and words.

In her finding of the Messiah, "whole mountains of living" were capsized into a "sea of blessing" (64, p. 15).

The woman received relief and comfort from Jesus. Whether her sufferings were the effect of the tragedy of being widowed five times or from the tragedy of a promiscuous life, Jesus knew, accepted, and had compassion for her.

In Jesus the woman saw a prophet. She raised the question of the place of worship—Jerusalem or the mountain, Gerizim. Jesus called her to worship "in spirit and in truth." He taught her that it is only in the Spirit that we can worship authentically as daughters and sons of God. It is this Spirit that continually animates and revitalizes a relationship with God in true worship. As a consequence, all that is obsolete, rigid, and meaningless collapses and falls away.

The woman had found the Messiah. "I am He." Jesus himself is the "living water" (John 7:37–38). His risen presence will be the new "place" of worship (Matt. 14:38). All other places, whether on a mountain in Samaria or in the city of Jerusalem, have given way to this new temple.

Following the encounter with Jesus, the woman left her jar behind.

Writing as he does in symbolic terms, John is telling us that the leaving behind of her jar is indicative of a deeper letting-go experience that had occurred within the woman. In Jesus she had found an authenticity of life. In the strength of this discovery, she was empowered to let go of limiting and empty forms of life and religion.

True to the dynamic of the Spirit, she hurried to share with others her marvelous experience at the well.

However, the townspeople of Sychar, as ourselves, could not believe simply on the message of another. "As a doe longs for running springs" (Ps. 42:1), we, too, thirst for God, and we must go to the deep spring within ourselves to meet and discover for ourselves the living water, the Spirit of Jesus.

And Jesus responds to our longing, saying, "It is already done. I am the Alpha and the Omega, the Beginning and the End. I will give water from the well of life free to anybody who is thirsty; . . . (Rev. 21:6).

Suggested Approach to Prayer: The Spring Within

+ *Daily prayer pattern:* (See pages 1 and 2.)
    I quiet myself and relax in the presence of God.
    I declare my dependency on God.

+ *Grace:* I ask for a deepening knowledge of Jesus and an appreciation for his humanity; I pray that I may love and follow him with growing intimacy.

+ *Method:* Contemplation, as on page 3 and Mantra, as on page 4.

I quiet myself and rest in the presence of God my Creator.

I enter deeply within the center of my being. I image, at the center, a spring of water bubbling gently. I see this water gradually rising up within me, flowing throughout my entire self.

I image the water bringing to every part of myself a fresh, cleansing energy of life.

I allow this gentle flow of water to move within my spirit.

I hear Jesus say repeatedly, "I am the living water."

+ *Closing:* I ask Mary to intercede for me that I would receive the gift of total dependency on God. I ask that I would be so detached from all things that I would put all my talents, possessions, and achievements at the service of Christ. I pray to follow in the pattern of Christ's life—even to the end. Providing it would not be sinful on anyone's part, I pray that if it is God's wish for me, I would have, like Christ, the courage and strength to endure poverty and/or personal humiliation.

I pray the Hail Mary.

In the company of Mary, I approach Jesus and offer the same prayer, that he would obtain these graces for me from my Creator. I pray "Soul of Christ," p. 141.

In the presence of Jesus and Mary, and offered by them, I approach God my Creator. Again I make the same request.

I pray the Our Father.

+ *Review of Prayer:* I record in my journal the thoughts and feelings that surfaced during my prayer.

Week V, Day 4: Repetition

Suggested Approach to Prayer

+ *Daily prayer pattern:* (See pages 1 and 2.)
  I quiet myself and relax in the presence of God.
  I declare my dependency on God.

+ *Grace:* I ask to know Jesus more intimately, to love him more deeply, and to follow him more closely.

+ *Method:* Repetition, as on page 6.
  In preparation, I review my previous prayer periods by reading my journal since the last repetition day. I select for my repetition the period of prayer in which I was most deeply moved or the one in which I experienced a lack of emotional response. I use the method with which I approached the passage initially. I open myself to hear again God's word to me in that particular passage.

+ *Review of Prayer:* I write in my journal any feelings, experiences, or insights that have surfaced in this "second listening."

Week V, Day 5: Love Responds

JOHN 15:12

Love one another, as I have loved you.

The scene opens. A middle aged couple are sitting in their favorite chairs, indulging in a piece of frosted, white cake and ice cream. Their manner is one of delight, nostalgia, and exhaustion. All around them are the remnants of a family celebration—left-over cake, wrapping paper, ribbons, and gifts of silver.

The wife looks at the pictures on the mantle, pictures of her husband and herself on their wedding day twenty-five years ago.

She: Wasn't it wonderful of Jayne to dig out those pictures for us. (looking at him) You know . . . you still make my heart "flip."

He: (with a smile) It *was* nice of the kids to do all they did. Remember all the times we worried that they would never grow up?

She: But they have, and they are so sensitive and beautiful. That has made it all worthwhile.

He: You've made it all worthwhile.

She: I still remember how I felt at the moment that picture was taken. I knew you would always be at my side no matter what happened. And you have been.

He: That's been mutual. . . . This morning I was looking at Bob and Laura with their children. They really do have a handful! And Bob—he isn't all that secure in his job. It brought to mind the years you and I faced that same thing. I really worried about money, but you were such a good manager.

She: I was thinking about those years, too. It was hard when the babies were small and dragging on me all the time. But you always seemed to understand and did what you could to relieve me. I still remember the times when we would go away for the weekend, just the two of us.

He: (laughing) We probably only did that once.

She: (serious) Yes, but I remember . . . and the times, too, when you were tired and would have preferred to stay home and watch television, yet we went out because you saw I needed to get away for a bit.

He: The hardest time for me was when I thought I was going to lose you. There isn't a day I don't thank God that they got it all.

116

She: (tears in her eyes) I was so scared! I don't know what I would have done without you then. I felt as if I had lost something of my self when they took my breast. But you've always made me feel whole and beautiful.

He: You *are* beautiful.

What we overhear in the dialogue is a tender remembrance of moments that have made up the fabric of a love that has been faithful, caring, and shared.

Each of the moments was rooted in a basic steadfast faithfulness. The couple had complete trust that they would always be there for each other. They remembered the long moments of deep concern for each other and for their children which had required a sacrifice of their own self-interest. There was, also, the memory of those closest moments in which they, in a mysterious oneness, had shared even the pain of the other.

This three-fold loving response—faithfulness, selfless concern, and union with the loved one—is what Saint Ignatius speaks of as the authentic human, that is, humble response to Christ's faithful, caring, shared love of us.

We are invited to love as He has loved us.

Suggested Approach to Prayer: With Christ

+ *Daily prayer pattern:* (See pages 1 and 2.)
I quiet myself and relax in the presence of God.
I declare my dependency on God.

+ *Grace:* I ask to know Christ's love more intimately so as to love him more deeply and to follow him more closely.

+ *Method:* Meditation, as on page 3.
Using the following prayer, I consider my loving response to Christ—what it is and what I would desire it to be.

LORD JESUS
I pray that your faithfulness may be my own.

I beg that I may never deliberately break the bond of friendship that unites me with you and that I may always be faithful to those persons in my life to whom I am committed.

117

LORD JESUS

I pray that my loving concern and care of others will be an extension of your own.

May my own desire be to please you and to be true to God's particular intent for me. Free me, that I may grow in self forgetfulness and may always respond in fullness of love.

LORD JESUS

I pray that I may be so formed in the pattern of your self-emptying love that I will embrace unhesitatingly any sufferings, poverty, and insults, trusting that in them I may experience union with you.

Enable me to let go of any fear that would serve as an obstacle to this total surrender of self in loving response.

LORD JESUS, RISEN,

Empowered with your humility, may my thoughts, my words, my actions serve to contribute to the joyful birthing of your presence in our world.

+ *Closing:* I ask Mary to intercede for me that I would receive the gift of total dependency on God. I ask that I would be so detached from all things that I would put all my talents, possessions, and achievements at the service of Christ. I pray to follow in the pattern of Christ's life—even to the end. Providing it would not be sinful on anyone's part, I pray that if it is God's wish for me, I would have, like Christ, the courage and strength to endure poverty and/or personal humiliation.

I pray the Hail Mary.

In the company of Mary, I approach Jesus and offer the same prayer, that he would obtain these graces for me from my Creator. I pray "Soul of Christ," p. 141.

In the presence of Jesus and Mary, and offered by them, I approach God my Creator. Again I make the same request.

I pray the Our Father.

+ *Review of Prayer:* In my journal, I record whatever feelings, experiences, or insights surfaced during the time of prayer.

Week V, Day 6: The Heart of Paul

2 CORINTHIANS 6:3–10

We do nothing that people might object to, so as not to bring discredit on our function as God's servants. • Instead, we prove we are servants of God by great fortitude in times of suffering: in times of hardship and distress; • when we are flogged, or sent to prison, or mobbed; labouring, sleepless, starving. • We prove we are God's servants by our purity, knowledge, patience and kindness; by a spirit of holiness, by a love free from affectation; • by the word of truth and by the power of God; by being armed with the weapons of righteousness in the right hand and in the left, • prepared for honour or disgrace, for blame or praise; taken for impostors while we are genuine; • obscure yet famous; said to be dying and here are we alive; rumoured to be executed before we are sentenced; • thought most miserable and yet we are always rejoicing; taken for paupers though we make others rich, for people having nothing though we have everything.

The heart of Paul was the heart of Christ. His entire life proclaimed, "I live now not with my own life but with the life of Christ who lives in me" (Gal. 2:20).

The description of his ministry graphically demonstrates the enduring faith in which Paul lived.

Paul's "faith in the Son of God" (Gal. 2:20) gave him the steadfast patience with which he was able to persevere through every hardship. Virtually unshakeable, Paul's endurance—his fortitude—was the tap root of his ministry commitment.

The faith of Paul, "faith in the Son of God who loved me" (Gal. 2:20), was enfleshed in his own person. His love of others mirrored his own experience of Christ loving him. Paul's kindness, purity of heart, and integrity was, in faith, that of Christ.

Subjected to suffering the contradictions inflicted on those who make the difficult choice to loving without compromise or condition, Paul was strengthened by his confidence in the "Son of God . . . who sacrificed himself for my sake" (Gal. 2:20).

In his total surrender of self to Christ, Paul experienced the paradox of having given all and having received "everything."

The heart of Paul had become the heart of Christ.

Suggested Approach to Prayer: With Christ

+ *Daily prayer pattern:* (See pages 1 and 2.)
  I quiet myself and relax in the presence of God.
  I declare my dependency on God.

+ *Grace:* I ask to know Christ's love more intimately so as to love him more deeply and to follow him more closely.

+ *Method:*
  I use again the approach to prayer "with Christ,"suggested on page 117.

Courage!
It is I!
Do not be afraid. Mt 14:28

Week VI, Day 1: Miracle of Presence

MATTHEW 14:22–33

Directly after this he made the disciples get into a boat and go on ahead to the other side while he would send the crowds away. • After sending the crowds away he went up into the hills by himself to pray. When evening came, he was there alone, • while the boat, by now far out on the lake was battling with a heavy sea, for there was a head-wind. • In the fourth watch of the night he went towards them, walking on the lake, • and when the disciples saw him walking on the lake they were terrified. "It is a ghost," they said, and cried out in fear. • But at once Jesus called out to them, saying, "Courage! It is I! Do not be afraid." • It was Peter who answered. "Lord," he said, "if it is you, tell me to come to you across the water." "Come," said Jesus. Then Peter got out of the boat and started walking towards Jesus across the water, • but as soon as he felt the force of the wind, he took fright and began to sink. "Lord! Save me!" he cried. • Jesus put out his hand at once and held him. "Man of little faith," he said, "why did you doubt?" • And as they got into the boat the wind dropped. • The men in the boat bowed down before him and said, "Truly, you are the Son of God."

The moment we allow self-doubt to enter our thoughts, we are, in effect, setting ourselves up for failure. Obvious as this may be theoretically, maintaining belief and confidence when one is overwhelmed by a crisis or buffeted by the threatening and contrary forces of life is very difficult. The first human response is one of fear and doubt.

So also it was for Peter. "As soon as he felt the force of the wind, he took fright and began to sink."

In precisely these moments, we are challenged with a choice. We can yield to the indulgence of self-doubt, or we can reach out to a power and presence greater than our own. Like Peter, we can cry out, "Lord! Save me!"

The unlimited power and presence of the Resurrected Christ is always with us. This is *the* miracle of the Christian Scriptures. "I am with you always . . . (Matt. 28:20).

In this highly symbolic passage, Matthew means to encourage the young, Christian, post-resurrection community to be constant in faith.

As the story was recalled, the boat was seen as symbolizing the faith community, and the raging storm was analogous to the waves of persecution that threatened it.

Like the disciples in the boat, the Christians were in danger of losing sight of the presence of Jesus in their midst and feeling alone in the "storm." Their faith would be renewed and their courage rekindled by the words of Jesus, "Courage! It is I! Do not be afraid."

As members of the contemporary Christian community, we, too, frequently find our own vision of the Risen Christ clouded by doubt and disbelief. Culturally disposed as we are to depend on the emotional tenor of our lives, we easily question the presence of Christ if we do not "feel" it. On the other hand, burdened with logic, we tend to deny or explain away the deeper reality of those graced moments in which we have a heightened experience of his presence.

The great challenge is, for us as it was for the early Christians, to trust in our own experience of the power and presence of the Risen Christ in our lives.

Only in trust does our vision become clear. In the moment of surrender, truth is seen, freedom realized, and authentic worship begins.

In trust, we open ourselves with all our brothers and sisters to the miracle of his presence as, in joy and thanksgiving, we acknowledge, "Truly, you are the Son of God."

Suggested Approach to Prayer: Walking on Water

+ *Daily prayer pattern:* (See pages 1 and 2.)
  I quiet myself and relax in the presence of God.
  I declare my dependency on God.

+ *Grace:* I ask to know and love Jesus more intimately so that I may follow him in faith and with courage.

+ *Method:* Contemplation, as on page 3.

I image myself in the boat with the disciples. I see the storm as it tosses the boat about, and watch the disciples try to bring it under control. I hear the howling wind and feel the salt water as it sprays over the sides of the boat.

I envision a figure coming toward the boat, walking across the chaotic water. I image the expressions on the faces of the disciples, their fear, confusion, amazement . . .

I hear Jesus say, "Courage! It is I! Do not be afraid."

I am with Peter as he cries out to Christ.

I hear Jesus say, "Come."

I consider my own response to Jesus' call. Will I leave the security of the boat?

I image Peter as he begins to walk on the water. I see him become fearful and doubting and begin to sink.

I image myself . . .

+ *Closing:* I ask Mary to intercede for me that I would receive the gift of total dependency on God. I ask that I would be so detached from all things that I would put all my talents, possessions, and achievements at the service of Christ. I pray to follow in the pattern of Christ's life—even to the end. Providing it would not be sinful on anyone's part, I pray that if it is God's wish for me, I would have, like Christ, the courage and strength to endure poverty and/or personal humiliation.

I pray the Hail Mary.

In the company of Mary, I approach Jesus and offer the same prayer, that he would obtain these graces for me from my Creator. I pray "Soul of Christ," p. 141.

In the presence of Jesus and Mary, and offered by them, I approach God my Creator. Again I make the same request.

I pray the Our Father.

+ *Review of Prayer:* I am particularly aware of my feelings, responses, and desires. I write them in my journal.

Week VI, Day 2: The Faithful Man of Jericho

MARK 10:46–52

They reached Jericho; and as he left Jericho with his disciples and a large crowd, Bartimaeus (that is, the son of Timaeus), a blind beggar, was sitting at the side of the road. • When he heard that it was Jesus of Nazareth, he began to shout and to say, "Son of David, Jesus, have pity on me." • And many of them scolded him and told him to keep quiet, but he only shouted all the louder, "Son of David, have pity on me." • Jesus stopped and said, "Call him here." So they called the blind man. "Courage," they said "get up; he is calling you." • So throwing off his cloak, he jumped up and went to Jesus. • Then Jesus spoke, "What do you want me to do for you?" "Rabbuni," the blind man said to him "Master, let me see again." • Jesus said to him, "Go; your faith has saved you." And immediately his sight returned and he followed him along the road.

Bartimaeus, the blind man of Jericho, was also the faithful man of Jericho. Bartimaeus was faithful in his need.

Blindness was a common affliction in biblical times, and it was not unusual to see blind beggars by the roadside. Often they sat near the gates of a city or town, their cloaks spread open before them to receive offerings from those entering or leaving.

Although physically blind, Bartimaeus was not without sight. In his blindness, his intuitive powers had become astute. Like all who live in shadow and darkness, he lived in hope, anticipating a time when "the eyes of the blind shall be opened" (Isa. 35:5). And in the approach of Jesus, Bartimaeus recognized the promised one.

"Son of David, have pity on me." His cry for compassion clearly indicated his awareness of the source of his hoped-for healing. His aggressive persistence in the face of the reprimand and disapproval of those around him revealed not only the urgency of his need, but also the depth of his belief in the power of Jesus.

Jesus heard Bartimaeus!

"What do you want me to do for you?"

Bartimaeus knew precisely what he wanted; he knew his need. "Master," he said, "let me see again."

Bartimaeus was faithful in his receptivity to Jesus.

Once called, he threw "off his cloak, jumped up and went to Jesus." Without a moment's hesitation and with total conviction, he hurried to receive his sight.

The years of begging and dependency on the generosity of others climaxed in that moment when Bartimaeus threw himself in "confident self abandonment" at the feet of Jesus (15, p. 46).

Bartimaeus was faithful in his following of Jesus.

No sooner had he received his sight than he chose to follow in the way of Jesus.

The readiness of Bartimaeus to pursue this way was in sharp contrast to the ambition of James and John, who lacked the insight that to follow Jesus was to offer themselves in a life of service. Their initial and primary concern had been to secure for themselves a first place in the Kingdom (Mark 10:35ff).

Bartimaeus, however, was motivated solely by his recognition of Christ. In Jesus he saw all he had hoped for.

We, whose "sight" is impaired in various degrees, are inspired by Bartimaeus to beg with persistence and confidence for Christ's healing power to touch and restore us. Only through faith in his healing presence are we given the consciousness that puts us on the road of discipleship to him who said, "I am the light of the world" (John 8:12). "I am the Way" (John 14:6).

Suggested Approach to Prayer: To See Jesus

+ *Daily prayer pattern:* (See pages 1 and 2.)
  I quiet myself and relax in the presence of God.
  I declare my dependency on God.

+ *Grace:* I ask to see Jesus, so that seeing him, I may love him, and follow in his way.

+ *Method:* Contemplation, as on page 3.

I image myself as the blind man sitting beside the road. I am aware of the scents and the sounds of my surroundings.

I ponder, recalling how long I have been blind and what it means to me to be without sight.

I consider what it is in me that needs healing and prevents me from recognizing Jesus in each person and event in my life.

I recall how I have come to know about Jesus. I reflect on the name I am most inclined to give Jesus when I pray.

I give thanks for the people in my life who encouraged me to seek Christ.

I hear Jesus call me to come to him, and I am aware of what I have to "throw off" to free me to go to him.

I hear and respond to Jesus' question, "What will you have me do for you?"

I image Jesus saying to *me*, "Your faith has saved you." I notice how I feel when I hear these words addressed to me.

I consider how the healing of Jesus motivates me.

+ *Closing:* I ask Mary to intercede for me that I would receive the gift of total dependency on God. I ask that I would be so detached from all things that I would put all my talents, possessions, and achievements at the service of Christ. I pray to follow in the pattern of Christ's life—even to the end. Providing it would not be sinful on anyone's part, I pray that if it is God's wish for me, I would have, like Christ, the courage and strength to endure poverty and/or personal humiliation.

I pray the Hail Mary.

In the company of Mary, I approach Jesus and offer the same prayer, that he would obtain these graces for me from my Creator. I pray "Soul of Christ," p. 141.

In the presence of Jesus and Mary, and offered by them, I approach God my Creator. Again I make the same request.

I pray the Our Father.

+ *Review of Prayer:* In my journal, I record the feelings and insights that have surfaced within me during this time of prayer.

Week VI, Day 3: The Touch of Faith

MARK 5:25–34

Now there was a woman who had suffered from a haemorrhage for twelve years; • after long and painful treatment under various doctors, she had spent all she had without being any the better for it, in fact, she was getting worse. • She had heard about Jesus, and she came up behind him through the crowd and touched his cloak. • "If I can touch even his clothes," she had told herself "I shall be well again." • And the source of the bleeding dried up instantly, and she felt in herself that she was cured of her complaint. • Immediately aware that power had gone out from him, Jesus turned round in the crowd and said, "Who touched my clothes?" • His disciples said to him, "You see how the crowd is pressing round you and yet you say, 'Who touched me?'" • But he continued to look all round to see who had done it. • Then the woman came forward, frightened and trembling because she knew what had happened to her, and she fell at his feet and told him the whole truth. • "My daughter," he said "your faith has restored you to health; go in peace and be free from your complaint."

"There lives the dearest freshness deep down things" (12, p. 70).

Up to this point, everything except this woman's gift of tenacity had failed her. For twelve years she had endured the humiliation and pain of continuous hemorrhaging. Twelve years of "doctoring" had not healed her.

As if the endurance of this physical affliction were not enough, she was also burdened with the alienation connected with the taboo against women who were menstruating.

This taboo marked her as ritually unclean and a source of uncleanness for others. At the risk of her husband's defilement, she was forced to forego any physical intimacy with him. In addition, she was forbidden to worship in the temple and was socially shunned (Lev. 15:19–30).

What enabled her to survive through those years of suffering, disappointment and loneliness? It may well have been the strength and resources she drew
upon from deep within herself. In the midst of such outward deprivation and
physical depletion, her journey inward must have been arduous, a dredging
search.

With all other options exhausted, her only choice would have been the courageous undertaking of this journey and the consequent discovery within of the
strength of her own goodness.

The reward of her endurance was wisdom. Out of the goodness of her inner
strength, the woman immediately recognized in Jesus the source of all goodness.

And this offered her a fresh possiblity of being restored to her own vitality.
Attracted as she was to this source and power of goodness, she sought nearness to
Jesus.

Jostled by the crowd, and aware of the restrictions of the taboo, she reached
out to Jesus. "If I can touch even his clothes, . . . I shall be well again."

At the touch she was healed!

In that moment the human and the divine met. In the synapse of faith, the
energy of divine power was released.

To the depths of her being the woman knew she was healed.

Jesus turned. He knew power had gone out from him; he knew he had healed.
"Who touched my clothes?"

In response to Jesus' persistent search for her, she came forward, trembling
and filled with awe. He called her out of the crowd. He called her out of any
residue of anxious self-concern or sense of inferiority. No longer would she be
hidden.

Released and freed, she must now claim her identity and role as a woman
made "whole" in faith.

Gratitude and joy filled her, and she fell at his feet. There, in her face for all
the world to see, was the radiance of new life, "the dearest freshness."

Suggested Approach to Prayer: The Healing Touch

+ *Daily prayer pattern:* (See pages 1 and 2.)
   I quiet myself and relax in the presence of God.
   I declare my dependency on God.

+ *Grace:* I ask to know the healing power of Jesus, that I may respond to him with a total gift of self.

+ *Method:* Contemplation, as on page 3.

I image myself as the woman who has suffered from a hemorrhage for many years and, consequently, has experienced disappointment, depletion of energy, and isolation.

I place myself in the crowd of people and observe the expressions of those around me.

I see Jesus as he moves among the people. I notice particularly his manner and his words.

I consider:
- what it is in me that needs healing; what it is that has been draining me of energy;
- how my condition has made me feel unclean, isolated, and alone;
- how it feels to be jostled and lost in the crowd;
- the efforts I have made over the years to be healed;
- my own deepest desire for healing.

I image myself approaching Jesus to touch his cloak.

I open myself to receive any experience of Jesus' power as I touch him. I become aware of my feeling response.

I hear Jesus say to me, "Your faith has restored you to health; go in peace and be free from your complaint."

I speak to Jesus from my heart.

+ *Closing:* I ask Mary to intercede for me that I would receive the gift of total dependency on God. I ask that I would be so detached from all things that I would put all my talents, possessions, and achievements at the service of Christ. I pray to follow in the pattern of Christ's life—even to the end. Providing it would not be sinful on anyone's part, I pray that if it is God's wish for me, I would have, like Christ, the courage and strength to endure poverty and/or personal humiliation.

I pray the Hail Mary.

In the company of Mary, I approach Jesus and offer the same prayer, that he would obtain these graces for me from my Creator. I pray "Soul of Christ," p. 141.

In the presence of Jesus and Mary, and offered by them, I approach God my Creator. Again I make the same request.

I pray the Our Father.

+ *Review of Prayer:* In my journal, I record the words that touched me, the feelings that surfaced during my prayer.

Week VI, Day 4: Welcoming Christ

LUKE 10:38–42

In the course of their journey he came to a village, and a woman named Martha welcomed him into her house. • She had a sister called Mary, who sat down at the Lord's feet and listened to him speaking. • Now Martha who was distracted with all the serving said, "Lord, do you not care that my sister is leaving me to do the serving all by myself? Please tell her to help me." • But the Lord answered: "Martha, Martha," he said "you worry and fret about so many things, and yet few are needed, indeed only one. It is Mary who has chosen the better part; it is not to be taken from her."

Wouldn't it be nice if Martha could come forward and tell us how she really felt in this incident? It would be wonderful—biblical scholars would love it!—since from the time of the Middle Ages, the passage has been generally interpreted in terms of the greater value and preference of the life of contemplation over and against the active life of service. As a result, Mary has been extolled as the model of contemplation, while Martha has been burdened with the negative implications of one whose life is less "spiritual" and occupied only with material concerns.

There is a side of Martha that we have not heard much about. After all, she did welcome Jesus into her home. That tells us something about her hospitality. Her anxiousness could be understood as an indication of the esteem in which she held her guest.

Meister Eckhart, contrary to preachers of the fourteenth century, presented Martha in a positive light. He saw her as a mature woman with a seasoned ability to translate her love into active serving of others. He interpreted her seemingly critical question, "Lord, do you not care that my sister is leaving me to do the serving all by myself?" as her concern that Mary would be fixated in the bliss of contemplation (32, p. 478ff).

However one may choose to look at Martha, the intent of this passage is not to pit contemplation and active service against each other but to point out that without prayerfully listening to the word, service is empty and becomes a compulsive, anxious striving. Mature disciples are those whose prayer and work are so integrated that they experience life as *contemplation in action*.

Their lives are a rhythmic balance of and continuity between prayer and activity. One flows freely into the other. Neither becomes a distraction for the other. On the contrary, they nurture each other.

To be a contemplative in action is to be simultaneously immersed in the reality of God and in the reality of the ordinary circumstances and practical demands of life. It means that our prayer, when authentic, comes to its completion and fulfillment in our total commitment to service of others. In turn, our service of others draws us back to God in prayer with renewed enthusiasm to receive again those gifts essential for our greater cooperation with Christ in the ongoing creation and renewal of our world.

The Mary and Martha within each of us invites Jesus within the "home" of our deeper self. We welcome the "Christ in whom alone the divine-human interaction is fully realized" (46. p. 1067).

In touch with God, everything we do is touched by God.

Suggested Approach to Prayer: The Visit

+ *Daily prayer pattern:* (See pages 1 and 2.)
I quiet myself and relax in the presence of God.
I declare my dependency on God.

+ *Grace:* I ask for the gift of deepening knowledge and love of Jesus that I may be in his spirit, a contemplative in action.

+ *Method:* Contemplation, as on page 3.
I prepare myself for prayer by asking for the gift of receiving and welcoming Jesus as he enters deeply into my "home."

I image myself expecting his visit. I consider what preparations I might make.

I am aware of my feelings as I anticipate his coming, for example, anxiousness, fear, excitement, hope. . . .

I image him approaching and entering my home.

I spend time with him, listening and responding.

+ *Closing:* I ask Mary to intercede for me that I would receive the gift of total dependency on God. I ask that I would be so detached from all things that I would put all my talents, possessions, and achievements at the service of Christ. I pray to follow in the pattern of Christ's life—even to the end. Providing it would not be sinful on anyone's part, I pray that if it is God's wish for me, I would have, like Christ, the courage and strength to endure poverty and/or personal humiliation.

I pray the Hail Mary.

In the company of Mary, I approach Jesus and offer the same prayer, that he would obtain these graces for me from my Creator. I pray "Soul of Christ," p. 141.

In the presence of Jesus and Mary, and offered by them, I approach God my Creator. Again I make the same request.

I pray the Our Father.

+ *Review of Prayer:* In my journal, I record the feelings and insights that surfaced during this time of prayer.

Week VI, Day 5: Repetition

Suggested Approach to Prayer

+ *Daily prayer pattern:* (See pages 1 and 2.)
I quiet myself and relax in the presence of God.
I declare my dependency on God.

+ *Grace:* I ask to know Jesus more intimately, to love him more deeply, and to follow him more closely.

+ *Method:* Repetition, as on page 6.
In preparation, I review my three previous prayer periods by reading my journal since the last repetition day. I select for my repetition the period of prayer in which I was most deeply moved, or the one in which I experienced a lack of emotional response. I use the method with which I approached the passage initially. I open myself to hear again God's word to me in that particular passage.

+ *Review of Prayer:* I write in my journal any feelings, experiences, or insights that have surfaced in this "second listening."

Week VI, Day 6: A Revolution of Love

LUKE 6:17–38

He then came down with them and stopped at a piece of level ground where there was a large gathering of his disciples with a great crowd of people from all parts of Judaea and from Jerusalem and from the coastal region of Tyre and Sidon who had come to hear him and to be cured of their diseases. People tormented by unclean spirits were also cured, • and everyone in the crowd was trying to touch him because power came out of him that cured them all.

Then fixing his eyes on his disciples he said:

*"How happy are you who are poor: yours is the kingdom
    of God.*
Happy you who are hungry now: you shall be satisfied.
Happy you who weep now: you shall laugh.

"Happy are you when people hate you, drive you out, abuse you, denounce your name as criminal, on account of the Son of Man. • Rejoice when that day comes and dance for joy, for then your reward will be great in heaven. This was the way their ancestors treated the prophets.

*"But alas for you who are rich: you are having your
    consolation now.*
Alas for you who have your fill now: you shall go hungry.
Alas for you who laugh now: you shall mourn and weep.

"Alas for you when the world speaks well of you! This was the way their ancestors treated the false prophets.

"But I say this to you who are listening: Love your enemies, do good to those who hate you, • bless those who curse you, pray for those who treat you badly. To the man who slaps you on one cheek, present the other cheek too; to the man who takes your cloak from you, do not refuse your tunic.

• Give to everyone who asks you, and do not ask for your property back from the man who robs you. Treat others as you would like them to treat you. • If you love those who love you, what thanks can you expect? Even sinners love those who love them. • And if you do good to those who do good to you, what thanks can you expect? For even sinners do that much. • And if you lend to those from whom you hope to receive, what thanks can you expect? Even sinners lend to sinners to get back the same amount. • Instead, love your enemies and do good, and lend without any hope of return. You will have a great reward, and you will be sons of the Most High, for he himself is kind to the ungrateful and the wicked.

"Be compassionate as your Father is compassionate. • Do not judge, and you will not be judged yourselves; do not condemn, and you will not be condemned yourselves; grant pardon, and you will be pardoned. • Give, and there will be gifts for you: a full measure, pressed down, shaken together, and running over, will be poured into your lap; because the amount you measure out is the amount you will be given back.

no time ago
or else a life
walking in the dark
i met christ

jesus) my heart
flopped over
and lay still
while he passed . . . (20, p. 455)

To genuinely encounter Christ is to have one's life turned topsy-turvy, upside down, inside out! To meet Jesus is to open oneself to a radically new orientation of life.

Jesus' message is universal, intended for everyone, not just for a chosen few. The power of his life continues to attract those who in their brokenness recognize a need for healing. Those who seek for wholeness find in his teachings of love and mercy the fullness of meaning.

His words give hope to our world. Paradoxically, he promises happiness and joy to those who experience poverty, hunger, grief, abuse, and rejection. Jesus blesses, not the misfortune, but the dependency on God that, by its very nature, suffering can create.

Those who are most empty have the greatest potential for receptivity to the fullness offered by Christ. This fullness of Jesus is the human expression of the mercy and love of God.

If we are to take the words of Jesus seriously, then we, too, must offer this "fullness" to others. However little we have, however empty we are, God asks for our total self. The challenge is demanding.

God demands our hearts. He "demands not only good fruits, but the good tree: not only action but being; not something, but myself—and myself wholly and entirely" (43, p. 246).

This call to love as Jesus loved is counter culture and exposes the superficiality of much in our world that disguises itself as love.

The most revolutionary demand from Christ is that we "love our enemies."

We are asked to respond to those who hate us, who curse us, and who treat us badly with a forgiveness that is unconditional and a compassion that has as its concern the well being of our would-be antagonist.

Faced with the evil of violence, love is the only viable option. Retaliation leads to the escalation of violence and to death. To meet violence with violence is to "make an unconditional surrender to its evil" (6, p. 104).

However, to meet violence with love is to neutralize violence. To love in this manner is to bring order out of chaos, life out of death. This is the revolution of Christ: the evolution of love.

This love fills our emptiness to overflowing. The mercy of God will not be outdone; it is the norm of our compassion. As God loves us, so we love one another. We love without condition, refraining from judgment, forgiving all injury.

We love, seeking no reward except the blessing of living in the Spirit of Jesus' forgiving, creative love.

Suggested Approach to Prayer: Prayer of Hope for the World

+ *Daily prayer pattern:* (See pages 1 and 2.)
I quiet myself and relax in the presence of God.
I declare my dependency on God.

+ *Grace:* I ask to grow in knowledge and intimacy with Jesus, in order that I may become a sign and a sacrament of his presence.

+ *Method:* Meditation, as on page 3.
I prayerfully reread the words of Jesus, pausing often to let them enter deeply into my heart. I listen for the call of Christ to me.
I thank him for the opportunity to hear his word.
I beg him for a full and vital share in the Spirit of his own forgiving love, that at all times and in all places I may speak and live in his presence.
I make an offering of myself to his service.
I pray the prayer that follows.

Prayer of Hope for the World

Lord God, we come to you in our need; create in us an awareness of the massive and seemingly irreversible proportions of the crisis we face today and a sense of urgency to activate the forces of goodness.

Where there is blatant nationalism, let there be a global, universal concern;
Where there is war and armed conflict, let there be negotiation;
Where there is stockpiling, let there be disarmament;
Where people struggle toward liberation, let there be noninterference;
Where there is consumerism, let there be a care to preserve the earth's resources;
Where there is abundance, let there be a choice for a simple lifestyle and sharing;
Where there is reliance on external activism, let there be a balance of prayerful dependence on you, O Lord;
Where there is selfish individualism, let there be an openness to community;
Where there is the sin of injustice, let there be guilt, confession, and atonement;
Where there is paralysis and numbness before the enormity of the problems, let there be confidence in our collective effort.

Lord, let us not so much be concerned to be cared for as to care, not so much to be materially secure as to know that we are loved by you. Let us not look to be served, but to place ourselves at the service of others whatever cost to self interest, for it is in loving vulnerability that we, like Jesus, experience the fullness of what it means to be human. And it is in serving that we discover the healing springs of life that will bring about a new birth to our earth and hope to our world. Amen. (11, pp. 7-8)

Appendix 1: Additional Prayers

Soul of Christ

Jesus, may all that is you flow into me.
May your body and blood be my food and drink.
May your passion and death be my strength and life.
Jesus, with you by my side enough has been given.
May the shelter I seek be the shadow of your cross.
Let me not run from the love which you offer,
    but hold me safe from the forces of evil.
On each of my dyings shed your light and your love.
Keep calling to me until that day comes,
    when with your saints, I may praise you forever.

(31, p. 3)

Letting Go

To a dear one about whom I have been concerned.

I behold the Christ in you.
I place you lovingly in the care of the Father.
I release you from my anxiety and concern.
I let go of my possessive hold on you.
I am willing to free you to follow the dictates
    of your indwelling Lord.
I am willing to free you to live your life
    according to your best light and understanding.
Husband, wife, child, friend—
I no longer try to force my ideas on you,
    my ways on you.
I lift my thoughts above you, above the personal level.
I see you as God sees you, a spiritual being, created
    in his image, and endowed with qualities and abilities
    that make you needed, and important—not only to me but
    to God and His larger plan.
I do not bind you. I no longer believe that you do not have
    the understanding you need in order to meet life.
I bless you.
    I have faith in you,
        I behold Jesus in you.

(author unknown; 72, p. 100)

Appendix 2: For Spiritual Directors

The passages and commentaries in this guide are keyed to the Spiritual Exercises of Saint Ignatius. The number in parentheses indicates the numbered paragraph as found in the original text of the Exercises.

For "The Principle and Foundation," see *Love* of the Take and Receive series. For Week I, see *Forgiveness* of the Take and Receive series.

Appendix 3: List of Approaches to Prayer

Index of Scripture Passages

*Page numbers preceded by a bold F are in *Forgiveness: A Guide for Prayer*, Take and Receive series.
**Page numbers preceded by a bold L are in *Love: A Guide for Prayer*, Take and Receive series.

Bibliography

1. Abbot, Walter M., ed. *The Documents of Vatican II.* New York: American Press, 1966.
2. Albright, W. F., and C. S. Mann. *Matthew.* Garden City, NY: Doubleday & Co., 1971.
3. Anderson, Bernard W. *Understanding the Old Testament.* Englewood Cliffs, NJ: Prentice-Hall, 1975.
4. Barclay, William. *The Gospel of John.* Vol. 1. Philadelphia: Westminster Press, 1975.
5. _____. *The Gospel of Luke.* Philadelphia: Westminster Press, 1975.
6. _____. *The Gospel of Matthew.* Vol. 1, Vol. 2. Philadelphia: Westminster Press, 1975.
7. _____. *The Gospel of Mark.* Philadelphia: Westminster Press, 1975.
8. _____. *The Letters to the Corinthians.* Philadelphia: Westminster Press, 1975.
9. _____. *The Letters to the Galatians and Ephesians.* Philadelphia: Westminster Press, 1976.
10. _____. *The Letters to Timothy, Titus and Philemon.* Philadelphia: Westminster Press, 1975.
11. Bergan, Jacqueline, and Marie Schwan. *Peace.* Privately printed 1983; available through Center for Christian Renewal, Box 87, Crookston, MN 56716.
12. Bridges, Robert, ed. *Poems of Gerard Manley Hopkins.* New York: Oxford University Press, 1948.
13. Brown, Raymond E. *The Birth of the Messiah.* Garden City, NY: Doubleday & Co., 1977.
14. _____. *The Gospel According to John I–XII.* Garden City, NY: Doubleday & Co., 1966.
15. _____, et al. *The Jerome Biblical Commentary.* Englewood Cliffs, NJ: Prentice-Hall, 1968.
16. Brueggemann, Walter. *The Prophetic Imagination.* Philadelphia: Fortress Press, 1978.
17. Caird, G. B. *Saint Luke.* London: Penguin Books, 1963.

18. Cowan, Marian, and John C. Futrell. *The Spiritual Exercises of St. Ignatius of Loyola: A Handbook for Directors.* New York: Le Jacq Publishing, 1982.
19. Crosby, Michael H. *Spirituality of the Beatitudes.* Maryknoll, NY: Orbis Books, 1981.
20. cummings, e.e. *Poems, 1923–1954.* New York: Harcourt, Brace and World, 1954.
21. Danielou, Jean. *The Infancy Narratives.* New York: Herder and Herder, 1968.
22. de Mello, Anthony. *Sadhana, A Way to God.* Saint Louis: The Institute of Jesuit Resources, 1978.
23. Downing, Christine. *The Goddess: Mythological Images of the Feminine.* New York: Crossroad Publishing Co., 1981.
24. Eliot. T. S. *The Complete Poems and Plays.* New York: Harcourt, Brace and World, 1962.
25. English, John. *Choosing Life.* New York: Paulist Press, 1978.
26. _____. *Spiritual Freedom.* Guelph, Ontario: Loyola House, 1974.
27. Fallon, Francis T. *2 Corinthians.* Wilmington, DE: Michael Glazier, 1980.
28. Fenton, J. C. *Saint Matthew.* London: Penguin Books, 1963.
29. Fitzmeyer, Joseph. *The Gospel According to Luke I–IX.* Garden City, NY: Doubleday & Co., 1981.
30. _____. *The Gospel According to Luke X–XXIV.* Garden City, NY: Doubleday & Co., 1985.
31. Fleming, David. *The Spiritual Exercises of St. Ignatius: A Literal Translation and a Contemporary Reading.* Saint Louis: The Institute of Jesuit Resources, 1978.
32. Fox, Matthew. *Breakthrough.* Garden City, NY: Image Books, 1977.
33. _____. *Original Blessing.* Santa Fe, NM: Bear and Co., 1983.
34. Gill, Jean. *Images of My Self.* New York: Paulist Press, 1982.
35. Greenleaf, Robert K. *Servant Leadership.* New York: Paulist Press, 1977.
36. Hall, Nor. *The Moon and the Virgin.* New York: Harper and Row, 1980.
37. Harrington, Wilfred. *Mark.* Wilmington, DE: Michael Glazier, 1979.
38. Heschel, Abraham J. *The Prophets.* New York: Harper and Row, 1962.
39. Houselander, Caryll. *The Reed of God.* New York: Sheed and Ward, 1954.

40. Houston, Jean. *Life Force.* New York: Dell Publishing Co., 1980.

41. Jung, Carl G. *Man and His Symbols.* New York: Valor Publications, 1964.

42. Karris, Robert J. *The Pastoral Epistles.* Wilmington, DE: Michael Glazier, 1979.

43. Kung, Hans. *On Being a Christian.* Garden City, NY: Doubleday & Co., 1976.

44. La Verdiere, Eugene. *Luke.* Wilmington, DE: Michael Glazier, 1980.

45. Lynch, John W. *A Woman Wrapped in Silence.* New York: Paulist Press, 1968.

46. McBrien, Richard P. *Catholicism, Vol. I, II.* Minneapolis: Winston Press, 1980.

47. McGann, Diarmuid. *The Journeying Self.* New York: Paulist Press, 1985.

48. McKenzie, John. *Dictionary of the Bible.* Milwaukee: The Bruce Publishing Co., 1965.

49. _____. *Second Isaiah.* Garden City, NY: Doubleday & Co., 1968.

50. McPalin, James. *John.* Wilmington, DE: Michael Glazier, 1979.

51. Magana, José. *A Strategy for Liberation.* Hicksville, NY: Exposition Press, 1974.

52. Maloney, George A. *Alone with the Alone.* Notre Dame, IN: Ave Maria Press, 1982.

53. Meier, John P. *Matthew.* Wilmington, DE: Michael Glazier, 1980.

54. National Conference of Catholic Bishops. *The Sacramentary.* New York: Catholic Books Publishing Co., 1974.

55. Neumann, Erick. *The Great Mother.* Princeton, NJ: Princeton University Press, 1963.

56. Nineham, D. E. *Mark.* Baltimore: Penguin Books, 1963.

57. Osiek, Carolyn. *Galatians.* Wilmington, DE: Michael Glazier, 1980.

58. Paoli, Arturo. *Freedom to Be Free.* Maryknoll, NY: Orbis Books, 1973.

59. Pennington, M. Basil. *Centering Prayer.* Garden City, NY: Image Books, 1982.

60. Rahner, Karl. *Foundations of Christian Faith.* New York: The Seabury Press, 1978.

61. _____. *Spiritual Exercises.* New York: Herder and Herder, 1956.

62. Rollings, Wayne G. *Jung and the Bible.* Atlanta: John Knox Press, 1983.

63. Sanford, John A. *The Kingdom Within.* New York: Paulist Press, 1970.
64. _____, and Paula Sanford. *The Elijah Task.* Plainfield, NJ: Logos International, 1977.
65. Scullion, John. *Isaiah 40–66.* Wilmington, DE: Michael Glazier, 1982.
66. Stanley, David M. *A Modern Spiritual Approach to the Spiritual Exercises.* Saint Louis: The Institute of Jesuit Resources, 1971.
67. Tannehill, Robert C. *A Mirror for Disciples: A Study of the Gospel of Mark.* Nashville: Disciples Resources, 1977.
68. Taylor, Vincent. *The Gospel According to St. Mark.* New York: St. Martin's Press, 1966.
69. Teilhard de Chardin, Pierre. *The Divine Milieu.* New York: Harper and Row, 1966.
70. Ulanov, Ann Belford. *The Feminine in Jungian Psychology and in Christian Theology.* Evanston, IL: Northwestern University Press, 1971.
71. van der Vaart Smit, H. W. *Born in Bethlehem.* Baltimore: Helicon Press, 1963.
72. Veltri, John. *Orientations, Vol. I: A Collection of Helps for Prayer.* Guelph, Ontario: Loyola House, 1979.
73. _____. *Orientations, Vol. II: Annotation 19: Tentative Edition.* Guelph, Ontario: Loyola House, 1981.
74. von Franz, Marie-Louise. *Projection and Re-Collection in Jungian Psychology.* La Salle, IL: Open Court Publishing Co., 1980.

To Our Readers:

It would be helpful to us, as we prepare to write the subsequent volumes of this series of guides for prayer, if you would be willing to respond to the following questions, and send your response to us.

Thank You.

Jacqueline
Marie

_ _

Please check the appropriate answers and add your comments.

1. I used the guide for prayer
   _____ regularly over a period of _____ (weeks or months).
   _____ irregularly.
   Comment:

2. I found the format (i.e., cover design, paper, type, layout)
   _____ helpful to my prayer.
   _____ unhelpful to my prayer.
   Comment:

3. I found the commentaries
   _____ helpful for entering into prayer.
   _____ difficult to understand.
   Comment:

4. The commentaries that were most helpful were on pages _____
   _____

5. I (used or did not use) the approaches to prayer.
   Comment:

6. What I liked best about the guide for prayer is _____
   _____
   _____

7. The following changes or additions would make the guide for prayer more helpful: _____
   _____

_____
(Signature optional)

Mail to Center for Christian Renewal at Jesuit Retreat House, 4800 Fahrnwald Road, Oshkosh, WI 54901.